D0555513

The Hymn Texts of Alan Gaunt

Stainer & Bell

First published in 1991 by
Stainer & Bell Limited, PO Box 110, Victoria House, 23 Gruneisen Road,
London, N3 1DZ, England

British Library Cataloguing in Publication Data
Gaunt, Alan
    The hymn texts of Alan Gaunt
    I. Title
    264.2

ISBN: 0 85249 801 2

Contents

Introduction

The name of Alan Gaunt is associated in the mind of those using contemporary collections of hymns with one or two strong texts, such as 'We pray for peace' *(24)* and 'Lord Christ, we praise your sacrifice' *(13)*. Such writing does not come out of the blue. It should come as no surprise that he is author of a whole corpus of interesting texts, such as would enrich the worship of most of our churches.

Like all the best hymn writers he is strongly biblical in his approach, though as is natural in the present situation with many translations and paraphrases of the bible in use, this does not come out in tags of scripture that can be immediately recognised in the text. He is prepared to look at bible, faith and contemporary world squarely and to bring them together into texts that can be part of worship. Thus he can deal with ecological concerns and the world's need of justice and peace without succumbing to the temptation of simply complaining in verse about what people are doing.

What may surprise some who know Alan Gaunt's work is the number of new translations of classic texts he has made. This is an important development in recent years. There are, it is true, many classic translations. Some of them, when one examines the familiar words, would not stand up in a modern collection in their own right. There are also new criteria that we wish to apply to our texts. We are no longer happy with excessive inversions or obsolete word-forms; we are learning to be sensitive to the fact that not all the human race wishes to be spoken of as 'man' or 'brother'. When we are dealing with a classic hymn of English repertoire we have to decide whether to alter the text or no. We are not so confined in our choice with translations. We can make new ones which may serve a new generation as well as the old ones did a previous one. Few translations convey the fullness of the original. A new exposure to the original through a new translation can be salutary.

Alan Gaunt stands in the great tradition of the English hymn in his use most of the time of traditional metres. For most of the hymns therefore the author is able to suggest a standard tune. To his suggestions from his own tradition have been added others from a wider field of choice. Sometimes he has in mind a new tune that is readily available, and this is referred to. There are printed here a number of new tunes. Some are in traditional metres and have been composed by people who have worked closely with the author, or who have responded to the element of the new in the text with a new tune. Where the hymn is in a metre for which there is no readily available tune a new one has been commissioned for this collection.

For the intention is that it should be possible to sing all these hymns. That, after all, is why they have been written. The new hymn book of the United Reformed Church in the United Kingdom *Rejoice and Sing* has a wide choice of Alan Gaunt's hymns, but even so cannot represent his full achievement. This collection of his complete texts so far is offered in the belief that many of them may well enter the regular use of the churches and many more prove to be exactly right for special occasions when a theme is being taken for which there is no hymn that is exactly right in any of our present books.

Alan Luff
Westminster Abbey 1991

EARLY HYMNS

1

8.7.8.7.6.

As we contemplate the future
set before the human race,
all the promise and the danger
of our search through time and space:
how can the mind keep pace?

Reaching out to seize the splendour
of a million worlds and more;
though we take creation's measure
and count every single star:
you, Lord, exceed them far.

And whatever worlds we conquer,
be it done through peace or war,
and whatever wealth we gather
from their undiscovered store:
Lord, we shall need you more.

For the universe is dying,
though it lives for countless years;
at the end of all our striving,
in the estuary of tears,
death comes to drown our fears.

But as you transcend creation
— spinning world and blazing star —
you have shown through resurrection
how supremely great you are:
death's only conqueror.

Lord, establish our devotion
through the days and years to come,
till we reach death's mighty ocean
and, baptized beneath its foam,
sight our eternal home.

Written: to Peter Cutts' tune BRIDEGROOM.

2   8.5.8.5.8.7.

Black or white or red or yellow,
people big or small,
child or grown-up, male or female,
whether short or tall:
each is different from the others,
but God's love enfolds us all.

We each have our special purpose
in the human quest
and, without the others poorer,
cannot be our best
till we find our life's vocation
in the love of all the rest.

So we greet the love of Jesus
by which we are shown
how to live our lives for others
as he lived his own;
by his perfect love united
we shall never stand alone.

He intends to make all nations
one great family,
shaping from our variations
glorious harmony;
then earth's praises, undistorted,
will resound eternally.

Suggested tunes: ANGEL VOICES or ARTHOG.

3

Come, living God, when least expected,
when minds are dull and hearts are cold,
through sharpening word and warm affection
revealing truths as yet untold.

Break from the tomb in which we hide you
to speak again in startling ways;
break through the words in which we bind you
to resurrect our lifeless praise.

Come now, as once you came to Moses
within the bush alive with flame,
or to Elijah on the mountain,
by silence pressing home your claim.

So, let our minds be sharp to read you
in sight or sound or printed page,
and let us greet you in our neighbours,
in ardent youth or mellow age.

Then, through our gloom, your Son will meet us
as vivid truth and living Lord,
exploding doubt and disillusion
to scatter hope and joy abroad.

Then we will share his radiant brightness
and, blazing through the dread of night,
illuminate by love and reason,
for those in darkness, faith's delight.

For the tune SUNSET (Stocks).

Author's note: This text seems to have become popular in a number of United Reformed Churches, since it was published in *New Church Praise*, and its first three words were used as the title of a record made from that book. However, no other book has taken it up. I have tried hard, for years, to improve the first stanza, but without success. But I am quite happy with the substantially altered stanza 5.

4   5.5.5.4.D.

God came in Jesus
human life sharing;
gave his life for us,
suffered and died;
then, Resurrection!
Death could not hold him;
by love's perfection
death was denied.

Then as they waited,
all of a sudden,
strong and elated,
freed of all cares;
with no misgiving,
joyful apostles
knew that his living
Spirit was theirs.

So let us greet his
coming among us;
let us still meet his
love with delight;
through resurrection
joyfully taking
love's new direction,
flooded with light.

He will be coming,
mighty and glorious,
universe humming
loud in acclaim;
through resurrection,
all of creation,
brought to perfection
praising his name.

Author's note: Yet another text for BUNESSAN, but see *Partners in Praise* 84 for DEATH DEFIED. Set to ADDINGTON in *Rejoice and Sing*, the new Hymn Book of the United Reformed Church.

5

Great God we praise your mighty love
which urges us to rise above
constricting doubts and fears;
your purpose is to set us free
to live our lives creatively
throughout the coming years.

We praise you for the love we see
in husband, wife and family,
in friends and neighbours too;
the love which nurtured us from birth,
the love which teaches human worth
and lifts our minds to you.

We praise you most for love supreme
which breaks through pain and death to stream
in unrestricted light;
which from Christ's resurrection dawn
has shone, and never been withdrawn,
to make our future bright.

For by your perfect love refined,
our own will not be undermined
by futile guilt and shame;
but through disaster, grief and strife
we'll reaffirm the joy of life
and glorify your name.

Suggested tunes: HULL or CORNWALL.

6 8.6.8.6.8.

God's Spirit strikes through time and space,
alive and giving nerve
to those who take their stand in faith
beside their risen Lord,
and trust their future to his word.

Our hearts and wills are stirred by love,
the love that turns all worlds,
that burns the countless stars and gives
each molecule its role
with all the rest, to make one whole;

The love that fills each universe
and overflows them all;
love, once compressed in Christ and killed,
exploding from death's night
in vaster, boundless, deathless light.

Invigorating Spirit, come:
keep us alive, aware,
alert to catch your spark, resolved
to serve your love and, through
our life's commitment, prove it true.

Urge us for ever on, beyond
the height or knowledge gained,
towards the peak, where we shall be
with Christ, our lives ablaze
with love and ever-mounting praise.

Suggested tune: HESWALL.

HESWALL   *Peter Cutts (1937 -)*

God's Spi – rit strikes through time and space, a –

– live and giv – ing nerve to those who take their

stand in faith be – side their ri – sen

Lord, and trust their fu – ture to ___ his ___ word.

7

8.8.8. with Alleluias.

Great God, now let your glory flow
in human veins, as once before
it did in Christ, made flesh with us:
alleluia . . .

Let us be wounded for the world,
your glory through our wounds revealed,
as once it was through those he bore:
alleluia . . .

Lead us through sorrow, pain and death,
and bring us back to life again,
with his own resurrection joy:
alleluia . . .

We come in faith to your delight,
facing the future bright with hope,
each one love's living sacrifice:
alleluia . . .

Here, as we voice creation's praise,
from hearts transfixed by Christ, we trust
praise will increase eternally:
alleluia . . !

Suggested tune: INCARNATION.

INCARNATION

Brenda Stephenson (1947 -)

Great God, now let your glo – ry flow in hu – man

veins, as once— be – fore it did in Christ, made flesh— with

us: al – le – lu – – – ia.

8   7 6.10 10.6.

In this world of violence, Lord,
how can we speak your word?
How can we ever work your purpose here
and live together, free at last from fear?
How can we speak your word?

There is violence everywhere,
more than our thought can bear:
spirits are broken, bodies crushed and bruised,
minds robbed of knowledge, dignity refused;
and people in despair.

In confusion, torn apart,
condemned before we start:
we meet within the hatred that we see,
within the violence and the tyranny,
the guilt of our own heart.

Here, before the cross we stand
and Christ gives his command:
'Love one another' — easy words to hear,
but hard to live by in the grip of fear:
We dare not understand.

Weak and by the cross deterred,
help us at all times, Lord
— engaged by love to take the risk of loss,
condemned to join the fight or bear the cross —
somehow to speak your word.

Suggested tunes: ARAKIE or SANCTION (printed on page 12).

ARAKIE

Paul Bateman (1954 -)

SANCTION

David McCarthy (1931 -)

In this world of viol – ence, Lord, _____ how can we

speak your word? How can we ev – er work your

pur – pose here and live to – geth – er, free at

last from fear? How can we speak your word?

9

6.5.6.5.

Jesus used to worship
in the synagogue;
with his friends and neighbours
sang his praise to God.

We, like Jesus, worship
in the church today;
still, with friends and neighbours,
sing our songs and pray.

When the service ended
Jesus took his praise
into streets and houses,
spelling out God's ways.

People came to Jesus,
frightened, hurt and sad;
helping them to worship,
Jesus made them glad.

Holy Spirit, help us
when this service ends,
still to follow Jesus,
still to be his friends.

When our neighbours meet us,
may they, with surprise,
catch a glimpse of Jesus
rising in our eyes.

Suggested tunes: EUDOXIA or GLENFINLAS.

10   8.7.9.7.9.7.9.7.

God is the boss, the poster said,
but I just don't believe it;
God will be angry, the preacher said,
but I just don't believe it.
We waited for God the boss to come,
to hail his fire and brimstone;
instead of that, a baby was born,
and where had God the boss gone?

You wait until he grows, they said,
you'll see how strong he is then;
he'll calm a storm and beat his foes;
but I just don't believe them.
He grows and people call him names
— Elijah or a prophet —
and Peter says, you are the Christ,
but I just don't believe it.

As, helpless in his mother's arms,
from Bethlehem he parted,
so at the end he's crucified,
as helpless as he started.
And yet his name's Emmanuel,
and that means God is with us;
Yes, God is helpless in the world,
and I just must believe it.

And so he points to you and me,
and to the strong and mighty,
and says you must be helpless too,
and throw your lives away, see.
Unless you're helpless in this world,
you'll never overcome it;
when comes the crunch, the strong are weak;
and, Lord, I must believe it!

Suggested tune: GOD IS THE BOSS.
Author's note: This was a response to a poster outside a Manchester
church, which read, *God is boss.* See also the note to No. **11.**

GOD IS THE BOSS

Reginald Barrett-Ayres

God is the boss, the pos-ter said,_____ but I just don't be-lieve it; __

God will be an-gry, the prea-cher said,_____ but I just don't be-lieve it. __

We wait-ed for God the boss to come, to hail his fire and brim-stone;

in-stead of that a baby was born,___ and where had God the boss gone?

11

8.8.8.8.8 8.

Lord Christ, we praise your sacrifice,
your life in love so freely given.
For those who took your life away
you prayed: that they might be forgiven;
and there, in helplessness arrayed,
God's power was perfectly displayed.

Once helpless in your mother's arms,
dependent on her mercy then;
at last, by choice, in other hands,
you were as helpless once again;
and, at their mercy, crucified,
you claimed your victory and died.

Though helpless and rejected then,
you're now as risen Lord acclaimed;
for ever by your sacrifice
is God's eternal love proclaimed:
the love which, dying, brings to birth
new life and hope for all on earth.

So, living Lord, prepare us now
your willing helplessness to share;
to give ourselves in sacrifice
to overcome the world's despair;
in love to give our lives away
and claim your victory today.

Suggested tune: RYBURN.

Author's note: This hymn began life in a totally different form as *God is the boss*, first published in *Dunblane Praises 2*. (See No. **10**). It has been used by more hymn books than any other of mine. The theme of the helplessness of God has always been important to me. I have developed my thoughts on the subject since these words were written, but they still express my convictions quite accurately. Lines 1 and 2 of verse 3 were altered by one hymn book committee, without permission, removing my deliberate stress on *then* and *now*. The same committee altered line 6 of the same verse, which read, *New life and hope for all mankind* to *humankind*, removing my deliberate emphasis on *all*. An illustration of the way hymn book committees can do violence to an author's thinking, when they alter to suit their purposes, without consultation.

12

C.M.

Jesus, we come at your command
to bring this child to you;
Lord, as you consecrate this life,
renew our own faith too.

We make the sacramental sign,
acknowledging your claim;
commit ourselves again to love
and service in your name.

We pray this child may see in us,
and all our children know
the wonder of your endless love
and in that love may grow;

That love which lived for others' good
and for their profit died;
the love which triumphed on the cross
and, dying, death defied.

As, with our children, we are called
your triumph to proclaim,
may we, like you, for others live,
our sacrifice the same.

Then, as a family of God
we shall fulfil our part,
till all the nations are baptized
and love rules every heart.

Suggested tunes: FARRANT or LAND OF REST.

Author's note: The original version of this was my very first hymn text, written c.1959 or 60. I wrote it and threw it into the waste-paper basket. About that time, I was looking forward to the publication of a small collection of new hymns. When it arrived I was very disappointed, especially with the baptismal hymns included. I decided that, however bad mine was, they were no better. I retrieved it from the waste-paper basket of the mind. A friend had it printed on sticky sheets, for his own church's use, and sold a number of copies to other churches as well. But no hymn book has ever taken it up.

13

7.6.7.6.D.

Lord Christ, your dying anguish
makes hope and joy for us,
and we have seen God's mercy
displayed upon your cross;
for where you were defeated
and shared our deepest shame,
we see, through death's cold darkness,
love's brightly blazing flame.

The world is still as cruel
and you're still crucified,
where human beings suffer
through love's demands denied;
despair and death still vanquish
both cowardly and brave,
and still our hopes and triumphs
are swallowed by the grave.

How can we stand uncaring
remembering how you cared,
or run away from sorrow
remembering all you shared?
Lord, where the grave has triumphed
and souls are in despair,
may we, your passion sharing,
display God's mercy there.

Cast off your earthly sorrows,
confirm love's victory,
and give us faith's perception
to pierce death's mystery;
then, watching at the grave-side
of human grief and pain,
we'll greet your resurrection
and share your endless reign.

Suggested tune: PASSION CHORALE also known as O HAUPT
VOLL BLUT UND WUNDEN or HERZLICH THUT MICH
VERLANGEN.

Author's note: This text was written for the congregation to sing at the
end of a humorous/serious play, written by me, called *The Gravedigger's
Fag*, which came out of a local Free Church Council's protest at
gravediggers smoking in the cemetery. Unfortunately, the play is now
out of date. There were some good bits in it!

14

L.M.

Lord Jesus, one you love has died,
we shall not see her/him here again;
and love is hurt and helpless now,
before the gathering grief and pain.

Yet, Lord, we trust your love for her/him,
far deeper than our own could be;
deeper than deepest depths of grief,
more sure than death's reality.

And so we put our trust in you,
acknowledging your claim to be
'the Resurrection and the Life',
love's meaning in death's mystery.

20

This one we love believed in you
and, though death has not passed her/him by,
still lives believing and, we trust,
believing still shall never die.

And, therefore, though we cannot see,
your words will sound through grief, to give
the light of faith we sorely need
to answer, 'Yes, Lord, we believe'.

Suggested tunes: GONFALON ROYAL or EISENACH also known
as LEIPZIG (Schein) and MACH'S MIT MIR, GOTT and SCHEIN.

15   A Wedding Carol   10.11.11.11.

Loving is dying: for you, love, I'll die;
loving is dying and being reborn;
loving is dying, as people apart,
loving is dying and rising as one.

Loving is giving my body to you;
loving is sharing your gladness and pain;
loving is risking myself to your fire,
fire which may hurt me as well as refine.

I am your phœnix, your bird of desire,
making my nest in the flame of your heart;
you are my promise of creaturely joy,
you are my earthly adventure and port.

Let us love on, love, and never despair,
looking to Jesus who turns love to gold;
day by day taking his cross to ourselves;
day by day shining, his light for the world.

He is our meaning that's too deep for words:
living with him we will fathom love's ways;
God's hand will touch us, the Spirit give nerve;
light of God's glory will shine in our eyes.

Suggested tune: SLANE.

Author's note: It is hard to imagine these words ever being sung at a wedding, but I like them.

16

8 8.10.8. and chorus

Moses was in the wilderness
taking good care of Jethro's sheep,
when he saw a bush that was burning bright
but stayed intact: a marvellous sight.
It was fire from heaven,
fire from heaven,
yes, it was fire from heaven.

Four hundred prophets cried to Baal,
shouted and bled to no avail;
but Elijah knew that his God would hear
his faithful prayer and send the fire:
Chorus

The king had died, Isaiah prayed;
he saw God's glory, felt defiled,
but his lips were touched by God's fire, then
he knew that he was clean again.
Chorus

When Pentecost had come around,
apostles heard a powerful sound:
it was the mighty wind of God which blew,
and with the wind came fire too.
Chorus

We've heard these tales of fire from heaven,
which really mean that heaven's right here,
and the Spirit of God still comes to say
that God is with the Church today:
In the fire from heaven,
fire from heaven,
yes, in the fire from heaven.

God, come and burn in us again,
to make us like your prophets then;
let us have the joy the apostles knew,
to set our hearts on fire too:
With your fire from heaven,
fire from heaven,
yes, with your fire from heaven.

© 1991 Stainer & Bell Limited

Suggested tune: MOSES WAS IN THE WILDERNESS written in
association with this text.

MOSES WAS IN THE WILDERNESS   *John Marsh (1940 -)*

but stayed in ⌐ tact: a mar–vellous sight.   *It was fire from*

heaven,   fire   from heaven,   yes, it was fire from   heaven.   heaven.

17   D.C.M.

> Out of eternal silence, Lord,
> you voiced the universe,
> and through the silent seeds of life
> you spoke us into birth;
> and out of silence, now the earth
> throbs with your mighty word:
> creation's vital pulse, by which
> life's energy is stirred.
>
> Our earthly silence is shot through
> with noises we have made:
> the roar of guns and bombs, the cries
> of those who are afraid.
> We should be still to listen, Lord,
> but in our faithlessness
> we fear the silence will confirm
> our own bleak emptiness.

24

But you have spoken through your Son,
your Word made flesh, through whom
you entered into death, to break
the silence of the tomb.
However deep the silence now,
in which we might be drowned,
there is no depth too deep for you,
no silence too profound.

Lord, though we harrow troubled earth
with strident, faithless fear,
still voice your resurrection life
and silence us to hear.
Deliver us from unbelief
and then, with joy ablaze,
we'll give your word fresh utterance
in faith's undying praise.

Suggested tune: PETERSHAM.

Author's note: I have often returned, in verse, to the concept of silence.
This curiosity was my first attempt to deal with the theme in a hymn. I
think it has its moments.

18   6.6.6.6.8 8.

Based on 1 Corinthians 13

Praise for the mighty love
which God through Christ made known;
love which for others lived,
died on the cross alone;
the love which heightens all our powers,
the love which makes the future ours.

Courage to face the worst
that people do or say;
eloquence, faith or skill,
fortunes to give away;
the means to feed the human race
or power to fathom farthest space:

Left unrefined by love,
all these are empty noise,
like instruments untuned
or useless, broken toys.
But he who died for love outlives
ambition's greatest victories.

Love makes the future bright,
transcending greed or pride;
life's possibilities
by love are opened wide;
and heights which seemed impossible,
by love are made accessible.

Love is the life of God
lived in our lives again;
this is the life for us,
worth all the hurt and pain;
and in the power of love we'll live
to greet the future God will give.

Suggested tune: LITTLE CORNARD.

19

8.7.8.7.

Praise to God, the generous giver
of the glorious universe;
praise to God for endless mercy
to the spoilers of the earth

Praise God's love, made flesh in Jesus,
not withdrawn, though stormed by hate;
crucified, yet ever living;
humbled once, for ever great.

Jesus calls us friends and partners
and invites us all to share
in the victory over evil,
planting goodness everywhere.

Though we cannot see the outcome
and must share his suffering too,
we believe that every crisis
yet shall prove his triumph true.

Praise to God, the victory's certain:
love has faced the worst and won;
celebrate the new creation
in the dying Christ begun.

Suggested tunes: SUSSEX or HALTON HOLGATE also known as
SHARON (Boyce) and BOYCE.

20   7.7.7.7.D.

Thank you, God, for Mary's child
coming like the rising sun,
with new promise and fresh hope
chorusing his matchless dawn.
Thank you, God, for each new birth,
each new person in our hands,
whose dependence speaks for you,
reasserts your love's demands.

God, forgive us: we have made
such a chaos of the earth
that anxiety and fear
mar the miracle of birth.
God, forgive our Babel sounds,
lust for power, religious strife,
breaking fellowship and peace,
sapping all the joy of life.

Speak to us in every child,
teach us true humility;
keep our hope alive, sustain
love for all humanity:
till in resurrection light,
peace restored and conflict stilled,
Christ will rise and shine for us,
all his promises fulfilled.

Suggested tune: HUMILITY also known as OXFORD (Goss).

Author's note: The original was written, *not* for Christmas, but on the
occasion of an act of thanksgiving and blessing in Christian worship
for Mondonna Karbaski — a Moslem baby. The first verse originally
read:

Thank you God, for this bright world;
every day the rising sun
brings new promise and fresh hope,
with the darkness passed and gone.

The last verse read:

Then, though sun may cease to rise,
all its vital light concealed;
you will rise and shine for us,
all your promises fulfilled.

21   10.10.10.10.

Sad clown with wounds, you gave your joy away
and brought new smiles to faces drawn with pain;
keen-eyed for truth, you pricked absurdity
but now, absurd, you hang pinned back with nails.

Red strands that flow from forehead crowned with thorns
stream down to meet the same from bleeding hands,
mingle with sweat to give your nakedness
a scarlet robe, fit costume for a fool.

And standing by are those who wag their heads
with cruel mirth and triumph in your pain;
your jester's eye aimed far too well for them,
they felt too close the arrow-head of truth.

Why don't you have the last laugh now on them?
Strip off the robe of blood, remove the nails,
and let them see this fool is not a fool
but God in flesh and their eternal Lord!

But no, Lord, stay: your last laugh is not here,
to make these few believe you for a day.
Your laughter soon will thunder from the tomb,
the universe be filled with endless praise.

Suggested tune: SAD CLOWN.

Author's note: This has never been sung by a congregation, but has
been effectively used as a solo in Good Friday meditations. When
Passion Sunday fell on 1st April in 1990, it was sung unaccompanied
and effectively mimed by a clown.

SAD CLOWN   *Alan Gaunt (1935 -)*

Sad clown with wounds, you gave your joy a – way   and brought new

smiles to fa - ces drawn with pain; keen–eyed for truth you pricked ab-sur-di –

– ty   but now, ab – surd, you hang   pinned back with   nails.

22   8.7.8.7.D.

Thank you, God, for other people
sharing with us time and space,
through whose presence you bear witness
to yourself in every place.
We can see you in each neighbour,
hear you speaking in each voice,
know in them your presence with us
when we suffer or rejoice.

There is one, who more than others,
shared your love and made it known;
gave us hope for life and dying
through the promise of his own:
Christ, who made himself the servant
of the humble and the small;
saw the value of each person,
gave himself, in love, to all.

Give us, God, his mind to see you
and to recognize your claim
to our deep respect and reverence
in the humblest human name;
let us meet and serve each neighbour
with the love we owe to you
and, without discrimination,
give to every one your due.

Suggested tune: CORINTH also known as BITHYNIA or ALLE-
LUIA DULCE CARMEN (Webbe) or TANTUM ERGO (Webbe).

23

6.6.6.6.8 8.

Based on Psalm 93

The great Creator reigns,
enrobed in light and power;
with God on constant guard
our future is secure.
Love reigns throughout eternity
in overriding sovereignty.

The ocean heaves and roars,
its battering breakers rage;
their thunder fills the skies
as endless war they wage;
but God outrides the fiercest storm
and in Love's presence all is calm.

Here, in this troubled life,
where we are sorely tried
by human grief and pain
from which we cannot hide,
Christ, walk the seas of our despair
and let us greet God's glory there.

Then, launching out with you
across life's angry waves,
we'll ply into the gale,
inspired by love that braves
the risk of death and total loss,
to prove the triumph of your cross.

Suggested tunes: LAWES PSALM 47 or ST. JOHN(S) (Havergal) also
known as ADORATION (Havergal).

24

We pray for peace,
but not the easy peace,
built on complacency
and not the truth of God.
We pray for real peace,
the peace God's love alone can seal.

We pray for peace,
but not the cruel peace,
leaving God's poor bereft
and dying in distress.
We pray for real peace,
enriching all the human race.

We pray for peace,
and not the evil peace,
defending unjust laws
and nursing prejudice,
but for the real peace
of justice, mercy, truth and love.

We pray for peace:
holy communion
with Christ our risen Lord
and every living thing;
God's will fulfilled on earth
and all creation reconciled.

We pray for peace,
and for the sake of peace,
look to the risen Christ
who gives the grace we need,
to serve the cause of peace
and make our own self-sacrifice.

God, give us peace:
if you withdraw your love,
there is no peace for us
nor any hope of it.
With you to lead us on,
through death or tumult, peace will come.

Suggested tunes: HERSTMONCEUX or REAL PEACE.

REAL PEACE   *Paul Bateman (1954 -)*

We pray for peace, but not the ea - sy peace, built on com -
- pla - cen - cy and not the truth of God. We pray for
real peace, the peace God's love a - lone can seal.

25   8 8.8 8.8 8.

We rise towards you, living God,
with our triumphant risen Lord,
who strides in glory from the grave
to take again the life he gave;
who leads us all a merry chase
through joy, hilarity and grace.

For death itself, so grim and sour
has been astonished by love's power;
infectious laughter from the tomb
has broken through its awful gloom
and, though it wears its grim mask still,
is forced to smile against its will.

And even to the depths of hell
Christ's laughter penetrates as well,
to touch the heart of deep despair
and plant the seeds of promise there:
darkness is light and anguish sings,
delighted by the hope he brings.

We'll come with him in buoyant faith,
through grief, disaster, pain and death,
his laughter ringing in our ears
dispersing all our doubts and fears,
until our joy is perfect too,
alive, Eternal God, with you.

Suggested tune: SUSSEX CAROL.

26

When sorrow withers human joy
and hearts are cold with grief and pain,
then we are summoned by our God
to breathe the warmth of spring again.

Our own joy may be withered too,
the cold may reach our own heart's core;
but we go on, compelled by love
and trusting to the spring still more.

The Man of Sorrows leads the way,
acquainted well with agony,
as through ice-cold Gethsemane
he passed, to die on Calvary.

Then, to his body, like a seed,
broken and dry within the earth,
there came the breath of God's own spring
to bring triumphant hope to birth.

And so we pass through winter's cold,
the hardening frost of shame and fear,
the long-drawn darkness of despair,
insisting that the spring is here.

No laughter, scorn or disbelief
will silence those whom God gives voice,
until his breath of spring has thawed
the last cold heart, and all rejoice.

Suggested tunes: TALLIS' CANON or HERONGATE.

27   6.6.8.4.D.

We praise you, Living God,
whose name encompasses
the powers behind the spinning worlds
and blazing stars!
We cannot comprehend
or fathom all your ways,
so far beyond the wit and skill
our mind displays.

Not ours, to take or leave,
to call or send away:
you come, you happen, as you choose,
the Great 'Ya-hweh'.
This name defeats our powers
of intellect and will,
and though we listen or refuse,
is uttered still:

As once it was in Christ,
humble and crucified,
in whom the world could see no power,
for he had died;
and yet 'Emmanuel',
'God-with-us' was his name,
and from the grave his great 'I am!'
confirms your claim.

Now let your Spirit come
to set our minds ablaze
with faith and hope and love, that fill
our lives with praise;
still set your children free,
as you have done before
and 'God-with-us' shall be our name
for evermore.

Suggested tune: LEONI.

LATER HYMNS

28   5.5.6.4.6.4.6.4.10.

WATERTOWN   *Peter Cutts (1937 -)*

Now Christ is ri — sen and it's time for joy;

time to be glad and sing and ce — le – brate;

time to let peo – ple know that life is good,

the world is won–der–ful, the fu – ture bright!

Now Christ is ri – sen, and we ce – le – brate.

Now Christ is risen
and it's time for joy;
time to be glad and sing
and celebrate;
time to let people know
that life is good,
the world is wonderful,
the future bright!
Now Christ is risen, and we celebrate.

Now we can play with
sun and moon and stars;
all creatures have their fling
and laugh with glee;
for God is laughing too
with such delight,
it shakes the universe
with ringing joy.
Now Christ is risen, and we celebrate.

Now crucifixion
is our sign of life;
Christ having died for us
can never die;
sorrow and grief persist,
but hope insists
we'll laugh and reign with him
for evermore.
Now Christ is risen, and we celebrate!

Written: c.1974.

Suggested tune: WATERTOWN.

29

L.M.

Revelation 19, 6-8

Help us to hear it, living God:
your praise from vast and roaring crowds,
like water rushing from the rain
or thunder crashing in the clouds.

Your crucified and risen Son
receives the Church to be his bride,
to share his life and spread the word
of deathless love, which loved and died.

The grace is yours, that led him on
to seize the final victory,
to make of death your captive slave,
the servant of your sovereignty.

Yours too, the judgement and the grace
that makes the Church love's fitting bride;
and ours the wonder and delight
rejoicing at the bridegroom's side.

He brings us with him, where you are,
to share eternal life and be
the sons and daughters of your love,
secure in time's uncertainty.

Responding to his summons now
to share his joyful company,
we join our voices with the throng
that praises him eternally.

Written: c.1976.

Suggested tune: JOYFUL COMPANY.

Author's note: The tune TRURO is a possible alternative to that printed opposite.

JOYFUL COMPANY   *Peter Cutts (1937 -)*

Help us to hear it, liv – ing God: your praise from vast ____

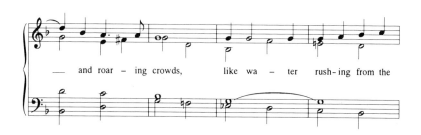

____ and roar – ing crowds, like wa – ter rush- ing from the

rain or thun – der crash – – ing in the clouds.

30   8.6.8 8.6.

Jesus, in dark Gethsemane,
in anguish and dismay,
keeping your watch alone, you weep
with your disciples fast asleep
Keep us awake, we pray.

Your only consolation there
— God's answer to your prayer —
the strength to rise and make your way
through deeper gloom to Calvary,
to fathom our despair.

There, at your grief's extremity,
in friendless agony,
heaven descended into hell
because in you God loved so well
guilty humanity.

Now, through your tears and deep distress,
your grief and loneliness,
faith contemplates God's heart and knows
the anguish love still undergoes,
to heal our wretchedness.

When we must shoulder our own cross,
Lord, join our will to yours;
though flesh is weak, help us to cling
to your nailed hands and, trusting, sing
the triumph of your cause.

Keep us awake, Lord, strong in faith
and let your Spirit's breath
strengthen our voices in your praise
through all time's hurtful, hopeful days,
and through the void of death.

Written: c.1975.

Suggested tune: BINNEY'S.

Author's mote: When I first sang Caryl Micklem's tune, GATES-CARTH to his words in *New Church Praise*, I felt that it could carry far heavier words. I had just finished reading Jurgen Moltmann's *The Crucified God*, and the first draft of these words came. It has been set in *Rejoice and Sing* to Eric Thiman's tune, BINNEY'S.

31

13 13.13 13.13 13.

For Tony Burnham

Great God, we stand before you as those whom you have called
to witness to your greatness and serve you in the world.
Our pride would gladly answer and modestly embrace
an honest reputation for courage, truth and grace:
but pride is not sufficient, it dares not pay the price;
it fears humiliation and shuns self-sacrifice.

And so we stand before you with him whose human name
shines out beyond all others, above all heights of fame:
Jesus, despised, rejected, by pride and unbelief;
disgraced, humiliated and overwhelmed with grief.
This is the Lord we follow, who suffered total loss,
yet lights the whole creation with glory from his cross.

God, keep us with the humble and give us grace to share
the struggles of the helpless who are your special care.
Teach us our place, as sinners, with those our pride condemns
and give us strength to stifle all proud and selfish aims.
Bring us where people suffer, to share their evil days,
until, with Christ triumphant, we sound eternal praise.

Author's note: Tony Burnham, a friend of long-standing, always enjoyed the tune, THAXTED, but never Cecil Spring-Rice's words. For his induction in 1981 as Moderator of the North Western Province of the United Reformed Church, he asked me to write some new words. Someone remarked afterwards, that the hymn was obviously an *occasional* piece but that he found the last two lines of verse two very fine.

44

32

For my son, Paul

Give us voice, our great Creator,
voice to praise continually
your unfailing love and goodness
welling up incessantly;
strike within us sparks of glory,
sparks to set love's joy ablaze
like a beacon in earth's darkness,
turning faithlessness to praise.

Risen Christ, our earthly brother,
sharing our infirmity;
for the joy that lay before you
facing death's finality;
in your human limitation
bearing love's authority,
now remain our joy for ever
in your deathless majesty.

Stay with us, eternal Spirit,
source of praise and power of prayer;
perfect stillness, spring of action,
conqueror of our despair;
in your presence we encounter
all the joy that heaven shares
in the living God, who calls us
as love's witnesses and heirs.

So we join the mighty chorus
sounding from eternity;
praising love's eternal glory,
one in joyful trinity;
all creation's expectations
surging into harmony,
soaring to their great fulfilment,
joy increasing endlessly.

Written: 23 May 1984.

Suggested tune: ODE TO JOY.

33

D.L.M.

Great God, your Spirit, like the wind
— unseen but shaking things we see —
will never leave us undisturbed
fulfil our dreams, or set us free,
until we turn from faithless fear
and prove the promise of your grace,
in justice, peace and daily bread,
with joy for all the human race.

Lord, shake us with the force of love,
to rouse us from our dreadful sleep;
remove our hearts of stone, and give
new hearts of flesh, to break and weep
for all your children in distress
and dying for the wealth we keep.
Help us prevent, while we have time,
the blighted harvest greed must reap.

And then, in your compassion, give
your Spirit like the gentle rain,
creating fertile ground from which
your peace and justice spring like grain;
until your love is satisfied,
with all creation freed from pain,
and all your children live to praise
your will fulfilled, your presence plain.

Written: 6 June 1981.

Suggested tune: PETERBOROUGH. Set to JERUSALEM in *Sing Alleluia.*

34

Revelation 22, 1-2

The stream of life flows through this place
and on its banks the twelve-branched tree,
with ever-ripening healing fruits,
fast-rooted in eternity.

Here, forced by pain to bend, we drink
the water from the stream to find
it quenches terror and creates
new strength of heart, new peace of mind.

We taste the fruits the tree provides:
compassion, grace and gentleness.
Their taste is love, with hints of joy,
to reaffirm life's blessedness.

Here we discern the truth of life,
which dawns through darkness, pain and fear;
and life's essential hope and good
receive fresh confirmation here.

The tree of life is one here with
the tree of death where Jesus died,
whose love asserts joy's certainty
though flesh is racked and crucified.

We do not trust to length of years
or to ambitions realized;
we trust this love, by hospice care
made flesh again and solemnized.

Suggested tunes: ANGELUS also known as DU MEINER SEELEN or ABENDS.

Author's note: This text was written in 1984 for the opening of St. John's Hospice, Wirral. A revised version for more general use is printed as No. **35.**

35

The stream of life is flowing here,
and on its banks the healing tree,
which bears its ever-ripening fruits,
fast-rooted in eternity.

If, forced by pain, we bend to drink
the water from the stream, we find
it quenches terror and creates
new strength of heart, new peace of mind.

We taste the fruits the tree provides,
compassion, grace and gentleness;
their taste is love, with hints of joy
to reaffirm life's blessedness.

We here discern the truth of life,
which dawns through darkness, pain and fear;
and life's essential hope and good
receive fresh confirmation here.

The tree of life is one here with
the tree of death where Jesus died,
whose love asserts joy's certainty,
though flesh is racked and crucified.

We do not trust to length of years,
or to ambitions realized;
we trust this love, by which God's grace
is still revealed and recognized.

Suggested tune: ANGELUS also known as DU MEINER SEELEN.

Author's note: This text, written in August 1989, is an adaptation for general use of that printed as No. **34.**

48

36   L.M.

1 Corinthians 11, 17-26

Corinthian Christians undermined
the truth of Christ by loveless rifts,
judged fellow members second-class
and boasted of prodigious gifts.

Dissensions at the holy meal,
the flouting of each other's need,
made love, the Spirit's greatest gift,
the victim of unbridled greed.

But who are we to censure them?
When we break bread, we share their shame:
remembering Christ, we justify
our separations in his name.

We too, deprive the poor in faith
of their entitled proper place,
as guests whom he invites to come
and savour all the gifts of grace.

While we remain unreconciled,
the nations, mobilized for strife,
are impotent to share earth's wealth
or set the seal of hope on life.

As we break bread, remembering you:
Christ, break us of our factious ways,
to serve your all-embracing love
and turn earth's poverty to praise.

Written: 23 February 1985.

Suggested tune: PITTENWEEM.

PITTENWEEM

Peter Cutts (1937 -)

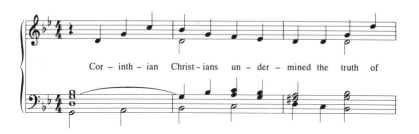

Cor – inth – ian Christ – ians un – der – mined the truth of

Christ by love – less rifts; judged fel – low mem – bers se – cond –

– class and boast – ed of pro – dig – ious gifts. praise.

37

L.M.

Based on Isaiah 49, 1-6

The prophet cries, 'Hear what I say,
take notice, people far away;
God picked me out before my birth
to shout his truth across the earth.

Must I become a nuclear blast
to make God's judgement heard at last;
its cloud exploding from the skies
to hide all mercy from our eyes?

I fear my faith is almost spent,
and earth remains impenitent,
and yet, with God, I cannot fail:
his love and mercy must prevail.

And still the Lord will have me say,
though earth and heaven are swept away,
the servants of the truth will rise
for ever glorious in God's eyes!'

So we must still remain God's light
to penetrate the earth's dark night,
revealing, with Christ crucified,
God's whole creation glorified.

Written: August 1985.

Suggested tunes: BERKSHIRE or DEVONSHIRE (Lampe) also known as INVITATION (Lampe) and KENT (Lampe).

38

11.10.11.10.

For Jan Berry

Eternal God, your love's tremendous glory
cascades through life in overflowing grace,
to tell creation's meaning in the story
of love evolving love from time and space.

Eternal Son of God, uniquely precious,
in you, deserted, scorned and crucified,
God's love has fathomed sin and death's deep darkness,
and flawed humanity is glorified.

Eternal Spirit, with us like a mother,
embracing us in love serene and pure:
you nurture strength to follow Christ our brother,
as full-grown children, confident and sure.

Love's trinity, self-perfect, self-sustaining;
love which commands, enables and obeys:
you give yourself, in boundless joy, creating
one vast increasing harmony of praise.

We ask you now, complete your image in us;
this love of yours, our source and guide and goal.
May love in us, seek love and serve love's purpose,
till we ascend with Christ and find love whole.

Suggested tune: HIGHWOOD. Set to CHARTERHOUSE (Evans) in *Rejoice and Sing.*

Author's note: In a discussion with my colleague, Jan Berry, we touched on the notion of the Holy Spirit as the feminine aspect of God. In isolation, of course, such a notion does not meet the questions raised by feminist theology. But if we understand the doctrine of the *Communication of Attributes*, this text does not, as other colleagues suggested, divide the Trinity, because anything that is said of one person applies to the others. The text was written on 25 August 1985.

39   6.6.10.4.

Life beckons, walk abroad
and grace fill all your days.
Display your faith's truth like the rising sun
and let it blaze.

Discerning grace at work
through all, in everything,
sing out your joy's truth in infectious song
to make earth ring.

Read parables of grace
in nature's energy,
to stir your hope's truth from a smouldering glow
to ecstasy.

Stride out! and though afraid
let every trembling breath
confirm your love's truth, through self-sacrifice
defying death.

Stride out with Christ, who died
to tame death's tyranny,
and find your life's truth blazing up in him
eternally!

Written: 13 September 1985.

Suggested tune: TOR.

TOR

Brenda Stephenson (1947 -)

Life beck- ons, walk ab - road   and   grace fill all   your

days.   Dis — play your   faith's   truth   like the ris – ing——

sun   and   let——— it——— blaze.

40 10.6.8.10.

We turn creation back to chaos, God,
by pride and unbelief;
our ruthless selfishness, rough-shod,
has trampled your creative joy in grief.

And must the climax of our story be
futility and pain?
Your love for our humanity,
all earth's potential: have they been in vain?

If, wasting earth to gain the mastery,
if, squeezing nature dry
for lack of love's humility,
we make the world a desert: we must die.

Already, millions of your children die:
the prey of war and waste.
We challenge you! We ask you, 'Why?'
You give your answer in the cross of Christ.

God, teach us how to read your answer there;
to realize love's price,
and find new hope for our despair
by working out our own self-sacrifice.

Then, peace with justice and your righteousness
will dominate our ways,
and Christ's obedience, found in us,
restore your joy and resurrect our praise.

Written: 5 November 1985.

Suggested tune: HUBRIS.

HUBRIS

Brenda Stephenson (1947 -)

We turn cre-a — tion back to cha- os, God,——— by pride and un—be—

— lief;   our   ruth-less self – ish — ness, rough–shod, has

tram — — pled your cre – a – tive joy   in   grief.

41

L.M.

How can we praise you, living God,
and celebrate this festival,
when millions cry for daily bread
whose hunger is perpetual?

Why do you let it happen, Lord?
Are we mis-led, to think you good?
Or are you helpless, after all,
to feed them even if you would?

Or is it we, so self-absorbed,
insensitive to poverty,
who block love's course and leave your poor
condemned to die in misery?

How can we praise you, living God?
— who doubt your power and righteousness;
whose greed and paucity of love
must make the earth a wilderness!

Great God, transform our politics;
restrain our ruthless selfishness;
by Christ's self-sacrifice in us
display your love's effectiveness.

May we yet reap love's harvest, Lord,
of justice and sufficiency,
and all be fed and spirit-filled,
with praise increasing endlessly.

Written: 19 October 1985.

Suggested tune: HURSLEY also known as GROSSER GOTT (LM)
and STILLORGAN.

42

Luke 4, 14-20

As once, Lord, in the synagogue
you made your purpose plain,
and had your neighbours all agog:
astonish us again!

Deprived, oppressed, your poor cry out
for justice and release,
and we, with them, must bring about
your just and lasting peace.

So fire our dullness, Lord, break through
our cool complacency;
let every eye be fixed on you
in thrilled expectancy.

In that electric atmosphere
enable us by grace
to see how love that meets us here
enfolds the human race.

Then, in that love's immensity,
we'll serve the world's deep need
and, armed with your authority,
be bold in word and deed.

And though we may be broken, Lord,
we'll brave these troubled days,
to seek the triumph of your word
in universal praise.

Written: 7 December 1985.

Suggested tunes: ATTERCLIFFE or EPWORTH also known as LOUGHTON (Wesley).

58

43   L.M.

Isaiah 60, 1-6

Why is the world in such distress,
when Jesus Christ has lived and died?
And did he not break free from death
to topple evil in its stride?

Reality can't match the dream:
the world is still sin's easy prey.
Where is the burning light of Christ
to blaze earth's wickedness away?

If Christians, overwhelmed themselves
by this world's guilt and misery,
still ask, despairing, 'Where is God?'
has faith become a mockery?

Arise! We must bestir ourselves
and shine! for if the world is dark,
we are the light of Christ today,
and we must be hope's vital spark.

Our faith is feeble still, and yet
we're like the star that marked his birth:
a point of light to guide the wise,
a pledge of peace for all the earth.

Where darkness gathers, we must shine;
where hope is stifled, we must dare;
and if our glimmer ends in death,
we'll fall as seeds of promise there.

Written: 4 January 1986.

Suggested tune: BRESLAU also known as ACH GOTT WIE
MANCHES HERZLIED or HERR JESU CHRIST (Leipzig).

44   7.6.7.6.D.

The world is full of stories,
of stories that have passed
to us along the ages;
great stories that still last,
to tell of human feelings
drawn deep from heart and mind,
more true than fact: their meaning
the surest we can find.

The world is full of stories,
new stories people tell,
and young and old come under
the story-tellers spell
which stirs imagination
and opens wide our eyes
to duty and conviction,
to wonder and surprise.

The world is full of stories
that capture and enthral;
but joyful faith discovers
that one transcends them all:
God's love as told in Jesus,
who shared our life on earth,
and human re-creation
beginning at his birth.

It tells us of the anguish
God's love was bound to bear,
to conquer death and evil
and fathom our despair.
As we repeat the story,
hope comes to life and thrives,
to make the love of Jesus
the story of our lives.

Written: 24 January 1986.

Suggested tunes: CLONMEL or ES FLOG EIN KLEINS WALD-VÖGELEIN.

45   8.7.8.7.D. Iambic.

Revelation 4

Around God's throne the rainbow shines
in lightning flash and thunder,
as each phenomenon combines
to fuel faith's praise and wonder.
On eye and ear pour noise and sight,
the flash and roar in fusion;
the light in sound, the sound in light:
astonishing profusion!

The voices, lights, the sea of glass;
fantastic beasts, all-seeing,
who fill the moments as they pass
with ceaseless praises, saying,
'The holy, holy, holy Lord
was, is and is becoming';
and all the elders, over-awed,
exultantly succumbing:

All these combined impressions, Lord,
remind us of your glory,
to be eternally adored
while we repeat the story
of your immense humility,
which shared our human weakness
and served creative majesty
through love's determined meekness.

Your glory, past all sound and sight,
pervades the whole creation,
and draws us on towards love's height
as faith's imagination,
unlimited by time and space,
joins that great congregation
which greets your turbulence of grace
with ceaseless adoration!

Written: 3 February 1986.

Suggested tune: GOLDEN SHEAVES.

46

L.M.

John 2, 1-11

On that third day in Cana, Lord,
faith sprang to being at your sign.
Can our faith's sparkle be restored,
like water turning into wine?

'My hour has not yet come', you said,
'What's this concern to you and me?'
But, by your mother, you were led
to share love's superfluity.

The servants took you at your word,
fulfilled their part obediently,
and so the miracle occurred:
the best wine flowed abundantly.

And yet your hour was still to be,
in which you would be glorified;
your mother then, in agony,
would watch as you were crucified.

62

Your dying pierced her to the soul;
she shared the price you had to pay
to come at last to love's true goal:
new life from death that new third day!

And should the hour come, when it seems
that hope for us is running out,
you'll conjure joy beyond our dreams
from grief, despondency and doubt.

We too will take you at your word,
fulfil our part expectantly,
to share your sorrow, living Lord,
and drink your wine exultantly!

Written: 25 February 1986.

Suggested tunes: VOM HIMMEL, HOCH also known as ERFURT (Leipzig, ?Luther) and FROM HIGHEST HEAVEN and FROM HEAVEN ABOVE or SOLOTHURN.

47
10.10.10.10.

For Graham Cook

Great God, you give the gift that each one needs
to serve the common good, and so to build
your new community of love and peace,
in which each one's potential is fulfilled.

But human ingenuity perverts
your Spirit's inspiration: we employ
the gifts we have for egotistic ends,
and foul with self the holy stream of joy.

Our institutions turn to monsters, Lord;
though made of individuals who feel,
they run amok, like dragons breathing fire,
devouring souls in their unfeeling zeal.

So, life for some is overwhelmed with things,
while others have no means of life to share;
and all, together, facing certain death,
are famished in the desert of despair.

God, give us then the gift of penitence,
and with it, truth and confidence to face
all earth's impossibilities, and still
to trust love's purpose for the human race.

For this, give worldly wisdom, too: the skill
to work the system, prompting change; to tame
our institutions by love's subterfuge:
love's just delight in each, for all, our aim.

Written: 30 July 1986.

Suggested tune: CLIFF TOWN.

Author's note: Probably unsingable, but as Graham Cook is famously
tone-deaf, that is perhaps appropriate.

48   11.10.11.10.

After Jeremiah 8, 18 to 9, 3

Stay with us, God, as longed for peace eludes us;
stay with us if our health is undermined;
when no good comes and faithless hope deludes us,
when terror reigns and grief is unconfined.

When consequence on consequence of evil
brings dreadful judgement on the human race,
stay with us, God, through torment and upheaval,
defeat despair with your persistent grace.

Yet grant no easy answer, no conclusion,
with which we might shrug off love's agony;
bring us with Christ through grief and disillusion,
fast-bound by faith to love's integrity.

Work out in us your love's determination
to bear your children's guilt and wickedness;
to harrow hell and harvest resurrection;
to forge creation's joy from wretchedness.

Written: 14 June 1986.

Suggested tune: ANSTRUTHER. Set to ZU MEINEM HERRN in
Rejoice and Sing.

ANSTRUTHER   *Peter Cutts (1937 -)*

Stay   with   us,   God,____   as   longed   for   peace   e –

- ludes us; stay with us if ___ our health is ___

un – der – mined; when no good comes ___ and

faith – less hope ___ de – ludes us, when ter – ror ___

reigns ___ and grief ___ is un – con – fined.

49

After Matthew 10, 29

No sparrow falls, so Jesus said,
outside God's tenderness;
no single hair on any head
eludes love's watchfulness.

To our restricted consciousness
it seems each creature's plight
to vanish in the emptiness
of life-negating night.

But Jesus saw the endless day,
where all that comes to be
can only ever fall away
to love's eternity.

And so he made towards the cross,
through grief and deep distress,
accepting death and total loss
to prove love's faithfulness.

Now faith constrains us to declare
that love, once crucified,
has plumbed the depths of earth's despair
and rises, glorified.

So, loving Jesus, keep us true
through doubt and questioning,
until we realise with you,
how love fills everything.

Written: 4 August 1986.

Suggested tune: ST HUGH (Hopkins).

Author's note: I do not know whether I was disappointed or pleased that such a simple statement should have come out of reading a passage in Karl Heim's, *The Transformation of the Scientific World View* (SCM 1953) pp. 157 ff.

50

10.10.10.10.

'Comfort my people, comfort,' says your God,
'speak to the heart of those who cannot feel
the measure of my tenderness for them,
or understand my eagerness to heal.'

Into your arms subsiding, loving God,
we found our darkness losing all its fears,
as death became a womb of waking life
and joy was watered by our bitter tears.

Against your gentle breast we laid our heads;
your arms were tightly round us, so secure,
until the hurt that brought us running home
became a blessing, making faith more sure.

Too immature in love to live in peace,
too weak to struggle on alone, we curled
as wounded children in your lap, until
you set us on our feet to face the world.

You ask us now to voice your tenderness;
to touch hard hearts that spare no love at all;
to show the weak how strong love makes them be.
We hear, and we must heed, your yearning call.

Written: 10 December 1986.

Suggested tune: HAYMARKET.

68

Author's note: I was attending a course on 'Sexism and God-Talk' at the United Reformed Church Windermere Training Centre. On the first night, I was not sleeping very well. At about 4 a.m. the first line of the second verse came into my mind, and I then went on to complete the whole verse, before falling asleep. It was after I had completed the next three verses, with the original as verse 1, that I felt I had to link it with *Isaiah* 40. The lines 2 and 3 of verse 4 were originally in the first person singular, . . . *I curled,/a wounded child within your lap . . .*

51   L.M.

John 8, 2-11

Teach us how grave a thing it is
to break love's laws deliberately,
to flout your holiness, great God,
or flaunt our shame presumptuously.

Have pity on our weakness, Lord,
and deal with us forgivingly;
but make us sterner with ourselves,
exacting strict integrity.

Restrain us from excessive zeal
in judging other people's sins,
for in our verdict passed on them,
your judgement of ourselves begins.

Prevent us throwing any stones,
aware of our unworthiness;
but, even more, remembering Christ,
who loves us in our sinfulness.

He routed those who came to vent
their fury in self-righteousness,
but bore their malice to the end
to perish on their bitterness.

God, give us his hard-centred love
to deal with human wickedness;
but make us hard on self alone,
contending for your gentleness.

Written: 1986.

Suggested tune: EISENACH also known as LEIPZIG (Schein) or
MACH'S MIT MIR, GOTT or SCHEIN.

52   L.M.

For Miriam and Martin

Each human person is, like God,
a dark, unfathomed mystery,
a hidden, rich, exotic land
across a deep dividing sea.

But love can span the space between
to make two spirits breathe as one,
within a bond that sets us free
and deepens as the years go on.

With firm commitment of the will,
we take responsibility
to seek for perfect love, which proves
God's image in humanity.

When life is glad, or full of pain,
in any clash of mind or will,
with feelings hurt or voices raised,
love keeps to its commitment still.

70

Through every duty and delight,
love shares the gift or pays the price,
till duty and delight are one
and joy completes the sacrifice.

Great God, when death brings grief to joy,
we'll come, through your integrity,
to find our promises and yours,
fulfilled in love's eternity.

© 1991 Stainer & Bell Limited
© 1991 Stainer & Bell Limited

Written: 10 September 1987.

Suggested tune: MORNING HYMN.

53   C.M.

Lord Jesus, as you broke the bread
for your disciples then,
confirm your presence now with us,
as we break bread again.

The bread we break still signifies
your body, as you said;
the wine we pour into the cup
still means the blood you shed.

As, one with our humanity,
in human hands you died,
faith sees within your brokenness
our nature glorified.

As we receive the bread and wine,
we come to realize
the promise of divinity
to which, with you, we rise.

And so, through this remembering,
we touch a depth of joy
which no intensity of pain
can fathom or destroy.

Lord, though we may be broken too
and come on evil days,
confirm us in your deathless joy
and turn earth's pain to praise.

Written: 1987.

Suggested tune: HITCHEN CAROL also known as BELLMAN'S
SONG.

54   C.M.

1 Kings, 19

We sing your praise, eternal God,
to whom all praise belongs;
but we can never match your love,
however loud our songs:

Your love which comes so silently,
through all the noise we hear;
the noise of quarrelling and war,
the cries of grief and fear.

The winds of doubt uproot our faith,
the earthquakes of despair
destroy our hope, and fires of hate
kill love and stifle prayer.

And yet no sound on earth can drown
the silence we have heard;
the voice of your eternal love;
the silence of your Word.

It comes to guilty, broken hearts,
with challenge and release;
prepares us for self-sacrifice
and speaks eternal peace.

Written: 18 November 1988.

Suggested tune: THIS ENDRIS NYGHT.

55

8.7.8.7.

We are coming into glory,
freed from guilt and reconciled;
each one, like the Lord of heaven,
God's uniquely precious child.

Christ, our Lord, for love's compassion,
once was born like us and died;
God's eternal Son, made nothing,
tortured, scorned and crucified.

Now he reigns in deathless splendour,
means to set us at his side:
heirs of his disgrace and sorrow,
reigning with him, glorified.

In this hope, his saints have served him,
facing danger, pain and loss;
we, though feeble saints, still witness
to the glory of his cross.

Through all danger, pain and sorrow,
through the earth's tumultuous days,
we will share Love's final triumph,
joining in eternal praise.

Written: 23 November 1988.

Suggested tune: MARCHING.

56

10 10.10 10.

After Julian of Norwich

Eternal God, supreme in tenderness,
enfolding all creation in your grace;
your mercy wraps us round, and ever shall,
and in your purpose, all things shall be well.

Eternal Son, as one of us you came
to be despised, made nothing, put to shame;
and now, a mother comforting, you call,
'All shall be well, and all things shall be well.'

Eternal Spirit, source of all delight,
you stream in glory through the soul's dark night;
we taste your spring of joy, for ever full,
and know within that all things shall be well.

Eternal Trinity, through grief and pain,
through all the malice by which love is slain,
through all earth's anguish and the throes of hell,
we trust to see, in you, all things made well.

Suggested tunes: SHELDONIAN or HAYMARKET.

Author's note: This text written on Christmas Eve 1988 reflects a growing appreciation of Julian of Norwich, which made me want to use *All shall be well. . .* in a hymn. The difficulty is to give it Julian's depth, and not make it trivial, as it is sometimes, for example, in the mouths of Iris Murdoch characters. *All shall be well,* but hell may stand between.

57

L.M.

Freely based on a Greek hymn for Good Friday

The Love that clothes itself in light,
stands naked now, despised, betrayed,
receiving blows to face and head
from hands that Love itself has made.

The Love that lifts the stars and sun,
collapses, spent, beneath the cross;
the Love that fills the universe,
goes on to death and total loss.

Love, helpless, comes to Calvary,
rejected, scorned and crucified;
Love hangs in shame, and dies alone;
but Love abased, is glorified.

Extinguished with the sun at noon,
Love's light transcends all history;
Love, wrapped in linen, Love entombed,
still wraps all heaven in mystery.

Though Love is lost, Love finds us here;
Though Love is absent, Love remains;
where Love is finished, Love begins;
where Love is dead, Love lives and reigns!

Written: 17 June 1989.

Tune: BELOVED.

BELOVED

Sue Mitchell-Wallace (1944-)

The ____ Love that clothes it – self in light, stands ____ na – ked now, de – spised, be – trayed, re – – – ceiv – ing blows to face and head from hands that Love it – self has made. Love is dead, love lives and reigns!

58   6 6 6.6 6. and chorus 5 5 6.6.

At all times, everywhere,
we are held in God's care.
God is Love, always there:
Jesus came to show us
love beyond a mother's.
Let our voices raise
songs of joyful praise;
for we know, all our days,
God's great love enfolds us.

Jesus lived here for us,
died in love on the cross;
now we gain, through his loss,
healing and forgiveness,
flowing from God's goodness.
Chorus

Now the Spirit of love,
coming down like a dove,
has assigned us to prove
Love's persistent good will
overcome all evil.
Chorus

God is Love, ever near;
Jesus lives; never fear,
for the Spirit is here;
though the world may break us,
Love will not forsake us.
Chorus

Written: 1 July 1989.

Suggested tune: THEODORIC also known as PERSONENT HODIE
(arranged Holst).

59   10.8.10.9. and chorus.

Philippians 4, 4-7

Now rejoice in the Lord, all God's people,
and rejoice in the Lord always;
through your gentle compassion for others,
help your neighbours to rejoice and praise.
Peace surpassing understanding,
guards our hearts and thoughts for evermore;
peace with Jesus, peace eternal,
peace from God whom we adore.

We will trust in the Lord, ever near us;
we will trust, and be unafraid;
we will trust, pray and praise, with thanksgiving,
we will trust and never be betrayed.
Chorus

We rejoice in the Lord, and are trusting
to rejoice in the Lord always;
we rejoice that, in spite of all sorrow,
all creation will rejoice and praise.
Chorus

Written: 28 July 1989 for the tune SING HOSANNA.

Suggested tunes: NEW BEGINNING (printed overleaf) or SING HOSANNA.

NEW BEGINNING

Paul Bateman (1954 -)

Now re – joice in the Lord, all God's

peo – ple,_____ and re – joice in the Lord al – ways; through your

gen – tle com – pass - ion for oth – ers,_____ help your neigh– bours to re-joice and

praise. *Peace sur–pass – ing un – der - stand–ing,*

guards our hearts and thoughts for ev – er– more;—   peace   with Je – sus,

peace   e – ter – nal,   peace   from God whom we   a –

– dore.

60

First three verses based on 1 Thessalonians 5, 16-23

Always rejoicing, ceaselessly praying,
constantly thankful, voicing our praise;
sharing the joy that fathoms all grieving;
glad in the hope that lightens dark ways:

10.9.10.9.

80

This is God's purpose, faith's expectation,
promised in Jesus, sealed by the cross:
joy that surpasses grief and elation;
hope that outreaches sorrow and loss.

Strong in the Spirit, facing earth's darkness,
we will inherit peace at God's side;
made, by Love's mercy, holy and blameless;
risen, rejoicing, with Christ who died.

Holy, Eternal, Love that creates us;
holy in Jesus, Love crucified;
holy as Spirit, Love that perfects us:
Love we adore you, Love glorified.

Written: 3 August 1989.

Suggested tune: MANY MANSIONS (INTERIOR CASTLE).

61
6.5.6.5.

Holy, holy, holy,
Source of all that lives,
Life of all creation,
ever be adored.

We who have our being,
Lord of hosts from you,
praise your love which keeps us
in eternal life.

Jesus, by whose dying,
we are brought to birth:
ever humble with us,
ever be adored.

Holy Spirit in us,
Wellspring of our praise:
prove our praise in service,
till all earth adores.

Holy, holy, holy,
Source of all that lives,
Life of all creation
ever be adored.

Written: 4 August 1989.

Suggested tune: MONTERREY or GLENFINLAS.

Author's note: These words were originally used as a sung response in the Eucharistic Prayer. See also No. **62**.

MONTERREY   *Paul Bateman (1954 -)*

62   6.5.6.5.

Holy, holy, holy,
Source of all that lives:
All-Enfolding Silence
of eternal love:

We who have our being,
Lord of hosts from you
praise your love which keeps us
in eternal life.

Jesus, by whose dying,
we are brought to birth;
ever humble with us,
ever be adored.

Holy Spirit in us,
Wellspring of our praise;
prove our praise in service,
till all earth adores.

Holy, Holy, Holy,
Silent Surging Love,
flooding earth with heaven:
silent, we adore.

Written: 12 August 1989.

Suggested tune: MONTERREY or GLENFINLAS.

Author's note: This variation of No. **61** was developed for use as a sung
response to the Eucharistic Prayer in another context.

63

8.6.8.6.8.6.

Our God, we praise your mother-love,
the love that gives us birth
as children of eternity,
who reach for heaven on earth;
and, precious in your sight, we praise
for all that we are worth.

When we rejoice your heart is glad
and all in heaven sing;
when we are hurt, your heart has room
for all the grief we bring;
you heal our wounds, you lift us up
and smile, as joy takes wing.

You set us on our way again,
and with parental pride,
you send us out to face the world
with Jesus as our guide;
to share your love and brave the storms
with him, who loved and died.

As children of your heart's delight
with heaven in our eyes,
uplifted on the Spirit's wings,
we joyfully arise,
to praise, to worship and adore
your love that never dies.

Written: 17 August 1989.

Suggested tunes: SHELTERED DALE or MORNING SONG.

64 Epiphany

7.7.7.7.7 7.

For Ruth and Raymond Clarke

In a world so cruel and cold,
one more woman, giving birth,
shakes assumptions, breaks the mould,
draws the love of God to earth:
in a helpless baby's eyes,
heaven takes us by surprise.

New born infant, powerless here,
precious in your mother's hands;
infant weakness, infant fear,
infant needs, speak God's demands:
all the powers of heaven rise
in a helpless infant's cries.

Though she marvels at her child,
pain must pierce a mother's heart,
if the *powers that be* run wild,
tearing those who love apart.
When a mother's offspring dies,
grief eclipses earth and skies.

Even so, through life and death,
Love sets hope against despair;
new-born cry and final breath
breathe out love incarnate there;
so the humble and the wise
worship where an infant lies.

Written: 30 November 1989.

Suggested tune: ARFON.

65   L.M.

Transfigured Christ, none comprehends
your majesty, whose splendour stuns
all waking souls; whose light transcends
the brightness of a thousand suns!

You stand with Moses on the hill,
you speak of your new exodus:
the way through death, you will fulfil
by dying helpless on the cross.

You stand here with Elijah too,
by whom the still small voice was heard:
and you, yourself, will prove God true,
made mute in death, Incarnate Word.

If we could bear your brightness here
and stay for ever in your light,
then we would conquer grief and fear,
and scorn the terrors of the night.

But, from the heights, you bring us down,
to share earth's agonies with you,
where piercing thorns are made your crown
and death, accepted, proves love true.

Majestic Christ, God's well-loved Son,
if we must share your grief and loss,
transfigure us, when all is done,
with glory shining from your cross.

Written: 6 December 1989.

Suggested tune: BROCKHAM also known as CONFIDENCE
(Clarke) and GILLINGHAM (Clarke).

66   L.M.

When people ruin people's lives;
when tyrants terrorize and kill;
when malice thrives and justice dies,
the silent God is silent still.

With children left too weak to weep,
or slain before their parents' eyes;
with hatred prized and life held cheap,
the silence swallows tortured cries.

When genocide goes unredressed
and innocence is racked instead;
with lies sustained and truth suppressed,
the silent God is left for dead.

Earth has no time for God who dies,
or those who suffer silently;
but looks for judgement from the skies,
to shatter ruthless tyranny.

But Love Incarnate comes through fear,
to stand beside earth's silenced ones;
Love's justice, overshadowed here
is brighter than a thousand suns!

Written: 1989.

Suggested tune: UFFINGHAM.

67   Dance of the Trinity

8.8.8.8.8 8.

We worship God in Trinity,
the One and Three and Three in One,
where three can never be a crowd
and one can never be alone,
for Love is One and Love is Three,
and shall be to eternity.

With one at rest, the three remain;
when one goes out the three proceed;
when one comes back, the three return,
for Three in One excludes all need;
and Love is One and Love is Three,
and shall be to eternity.

With Three in One and One in three,
where wisdom, love and power all meet,
Eternal Love needs nothing more
and peace and joy are here complete:
for Love is One and Love is Three,
and shall be to eternity.

And yet this Love has overflowed;
the miracle has taken place:
creation, Love's great enterprise,
has brought us into God's embrace;
for Love as One and Love as Three,
enfolds us in its mystery.

Suggested tunes: CHRISTUS IST ERSTANDEN also known as VICTOR KING, with the first crotchet changed to two minims or SUSSEX CAROL.

Author's note: These words were written on 16 January 1990 specifically for a weekend Liturgical Dance Course at the United Reformed Church Windermere Centre, and expressed in dance at Sunday morning worship in the Carver Memorial United Reformed Church, Windermere that same weekend.

68   7.6.7.6.D.

For The Windermere Centre

Adore the great Creator
and praise Love's Trinity:
Transcendent and Incarnate,
Eternal Mystery.
From this substantial centre, [1]
direct the loving gaze, [2]
to see earth crammed with heaven
and every bush ablaze. [3]

The lakes and mountains round us,
enhanced by sun and clouds;
the flowing screes and pathways
worn down by rambling crowds;
to faith, proclaim the presence
of God, whose endless grace,
in judgement fused with mercy,
enfolds the human race.

Earth's sacramental splendour
unfolds the searching Word,
and deep thought is invited
and deep emotion stirred. [4]
Here faith can ask its questions,
and doubt be entertained;
here love can claim its freedom,
and hope be unrestrained.

Here intellect is nurtured,
imagination fired;
the minds that have been settled,
the spirits that are tired,
confront disturbing insights
and face the bracing call,
to bear earth's toil and passion
and find God all in all.

Written: 19 February 1990.

Suggested tunes: MOUNTAIN CHRISTIANS or KINGS LYNN.

Author's note: A Hymn of *Wordsworthian Sacramentalism* written for
the occasion of the opening of an extension to the United Reformed
Church Training Centre, Windermere. Norman Nicholson wrote in
The Lakers:

> For though his philosophy may not be specifically
> Christian, yet I believe that it can only be fully understood
> in the framework of Christian morality . . . Wordsworth,
> then, belongs to one of the great Ways of Christian
> teaching, the Sacramental Way, or, in the term
> popularised by Charles Williams, the Affirmative Way.

By permission of David Higham Associates and Robert Hale.

[1] W. Wordsworth, *The Prelude*

[2] Iris Murdoch, *The Sovereignty of Good*

[3] E. Barrett Browning, *Aurora Leigh*

[4] S. T. Coleridge, *Biographia Literaria*

69   8.6.8.6.8.6.

1 Kings 17, 10-16 etc

If every crop on earth should fail
and every stream run dry;
if human life should waste away,
all comfort pass us by:
the source of hope would not run out
and love would never die.

The life of Jesus, once poured out
for all the human race,
now overflows the universe,
transcending time and space,
to be a never-emptied source
of God's undying grace.

Rejected once, and crucified,
now, risen Christ, appear
to show us your undying love;
to drive away our fear;
to be the sustenance we need
as your disciples here.

Make us your bread of life today,
for hungry ones to share;
the bread you break to feed the crowds:
sufficient and to spare,
till all on earth are satisfied,
with justice everywhere.

Written: 15 February 1990.

Suggested tunes: TYNEMOUTH (Choron) or SHELTERED DALE
or MORNING SONG.

70   6.6.6.6.8 8.

Eternal mercy wraps
the whole creation round;
when judgement overflows
and wickedness is drowned,
the fragile rainbow in its place
reminds us of enduring grace.

For love will not destroy
what love itself has made;
when we have done our worst,
when love has been betrayed:
there, at the depths of evil will,
we find God's love is deeper still.

The cost of love is great,
too great for us to bear;
the heart of God alone
can hold the world's despair;
and love incarnate at our side
is taunted, broken, crucified.

But, breaking free from death,
love demonstrates its worth:
its power to take away
the sins of all the earth;
and we, forgiven, prove love true
as we forgive our neighbours too.

Though evil clouds our skies,
and though afraid to drown,
we launch into the deep,
and tread the chaos down;
like Peter walking on the waves,
we fix our eyes on Christ who saves.

Written: 9 March 1990.

Suggested tunes: LAWES PSALM 47 or RALEIGH.

71

5.5.5.5.5.5.5.4.

For Winifred

After Julian of Norwich

Love is God's meaning,
love is God's reason;
love is God's glory,
love is God's shame;
love is God's sorrow,
love is God's gladness;
love is God's promise:
Love is God's name.

Love is our calling,
Love, our adventure,
Love, our beginning,
Love is our goal;
Love is our sorrow,
Love is our gladness;
Love is our breaking,
Love makes us whole.

Sharing Love's anguish
over all sinners;
pleading forgiveness,
we too can tell
how Love, beyond us,
human beside us,
living within us,
makes all things well.

Love will not fail us,
Love will not lose us,
Love's mercy reaches
deeper than hell;
Love will enfold us,
Love will release us,
Love will complete us:
all shall be well.

Written: 7 April 1990.

Suggested tune: MANY MANSIONS (INTERIOR CASTLE).

72 For All Fools Day   10.8.10.9. and chorus

In the times when our faith seems to fail us;
when our hope hits the sinking sands;
when our love is defeated and dying:
if we fall away, God's wisdom stands.
We are fools with Christ, made nothing,
weak and helpless with the one who died;
in God's wisdom, through our weakness,
foolishness is glorified.

Living God, at the dawn of creation,
as you laughed for the worlds begun,
you were grieving for evil and sorrow,
for the clouds that would eclipse your Son.
Chorus

Living Christ, as you stood with earth's victims,
made a fool of and crowned with thorn;
come and burst all the arrogant bubbles
of our prejudice and pride and scorn.
Chorus

In the Spirit, our faith will not fail us,
and our hope will not let us down;
each one counted with Christ in his folly,
is set up to be love's wounded clown.
Chorus

Written: 31 March 1990.

Suggested tune: SING HOSANNA.

73

7.6.7.6.D.

Too many things have hindered
our peace, dear God, with you;
in veiled and open conflict,
we know not what we do;
for, from the deep unconscious,
emerging storms and fears
have drowned our hopes of healing
in bitterness and tears.

And yet in Christ, beside us,
your love has shared our pain:
the grief, the hateful tensions,
the anger and disdain;
the one who came with healing
and set the guilty free,
himself endured hell's anguish
in grim Gethsemane.

Your love absorbed our anger
in Jesus, crucified;
and depths of death and evil
are purged and purified
as, through your Holy Spirit,
love fathoms mind's deep space,
to touch our hidden being
with resurrection grace.

Though we still cry for freedom
from conflict grief and sin,
your healing love surrounds us
and meets us from within;
we rise to health and wholeness,
our joy and praise increase;
for we are held already
in your eternal peace.

Written: 11 May 1990.

Possible tunes: ES FLOG EIN KLEINS WALDVÖGELEIN or BENTLEY or MUNICH also known as BREMEN.

74   6.6.6.6.8 8.

For Ethel Mary Gaunt born 11 April 1904 — died 28 March 1989 — with whom I came to know the Resurrected Christ.

John 20, 11-17

> Woman, why do you weep?
> she hears the angels say;
> Woman, why do you weep?
> 'They took my Lord away:
> the Lord I love so tenderly,
> and now, where can his body be?'
>
> Woman, why do you weep?
> she hears the gardener say;
> Woman, why do you weep?
> 'They took my Lord away:
> my Lord, so precious in my eyes,
> Oh, tell me where his body lies.'
>
> The empty tomb is dumb,
> and angels have no word
> for Mary in her grief,
> who seeks her buried Lord;
> she turns to find him standing there,
> yet fails to see beyond despair.
>
> But when he speaks her name,
> despair and grief have flown;
> she moves to his embrace
> and greets him as her own:
> yet must not cling to him, but go
> to let bereft disciples know.

Christ, with us, speak our name,
and fill our lives today
with resurrection joy;
then send us on our way,
proclaiming faith, which strides above
despair and death, in deathless love.

Written: 11 April 1990.

Suggested tune: LOVE UNKNOWN.

75

8.7.8.7.

Based on 'Revelations of Divine Love': Julian of Norwich Chapter 48

Here is God, the Holy Spirit,
endless life within the soul;
love that keeps us God's for ever,
endless peace that makes us whole.

Here is Love's unchanging mercy,
circling every soul that lives;
here we find no trace of anger,
but our own, which Love forgives.

Anger rises from our weakness,
rooted in our pride and fear;
but, when peace and love seem ruined,
still we find a refuge here.

In God's goodness, strength and wisdom,
hope still rises from love's ground;
in the pity of the Spirit,
tender mercy wraps us round.

Losing sight of God, and dying,
perishing in sin and strife;
caught up in the Spirit's splendour,
we are brought from death to life.

Though we face the searing judgement,
nothing can compare with this:
God's vast mercy, love's abundance,
boundless peace and endless bliss.

Written: 29 May 1990.

Suggested tune: ALL FOR JESUS.

76

7.6.7.6.D.

For Graham and Jean Cook

The rainbow of God's mercy
has over-arched the years,
creating joyful colours
from human grief and tears;
we see the dark clouds gather,
we hear the thunder roll,
then, suddenly the rainbow
elates the fearful soul.

As we approach the future,
not knowing what we'll find;
aware that storms of evil
could swamp all human kind;
the rainbow arches over
our ignorance and strife:
God's promise of forgiveness,
our gateway into Life.

98

God, let your light in Jesus,
love's pure white light ablaze,
diffracted into rainbows
through faithfulness and praise,
shed faith, hope, love and mercy
— the colours of your grace —
with peace, delight and justice,
on all the human race.

Written: 6 July 1990.

Suggested tunes: CLONMEL or OFFERTORIUM.

77   7.7.7.7.

Holy Spirit, gift of Christ,
come into our lives and stay;
in your overflow of love
carry all our fears away.

As we taste the broken bread,
give us Jesus crucified;
feed us with eternal life,
harvest of the love that died.

In our sharing of the wine,
let delight and hope increase,
as we greet the risen Christ:
present with us, breathing peace.

In the bread and wine, in us,
set the love of Christ ablaze;
filling all things, let it burn,
unconsumed, in endless praise.

Written: 8 October 1990.

Suggested tunes: HARTS also known as HARTFORD or MONKLAND.

Author's note: This was written to be sung as part of the Eucharistic Prayer.

78   L.M.

God's Spirit, as a rising gale,
tear down our false tranquility;
come surging through our settled minds,
demolish our complacency!

God's Spirit, as the breath of life,
creation's source and guide and goal,
breathe life into our souls again,
restore our faith and make us whole.

God's Spirit, as an icy blast,
strike through the scorching enmity
that burns our human love to ash;
extinguish all hostility.

God's Spirit, as a healing breeze,
stream gently through our troubled days,
to set us on our feet again,
with confidence, delight and praise.

God's Spirit, fierce and wild, and yet
enfolding like a mother's womb,
surprise us, bring us, newly born,
with Jesus leaping from the tomb!

Written: 23 July 1990.

Tune: ST. BARTHOLOMEW (Duncalf).

79   11.9.11.8. and chorus 6.6.6.5.

Called to one faith and receiving one Spirit,
we share one hope in the peace of Christ;
coming as sisters and brothers together,
we pray that the church may be one.
We all serve the one God,
known as crucified Lord;
in the Spirit of love,
endlessly adored.

Breaking one bread, we become the one Body,
The Body of Christ in the world today;
broken with him, for the love of God's children,
until all on earth are made one.
So we serve the one God,
known as crucified Lord;
in the Spirit of love,
endlessly adored.

Called by the Spirit, as signs of God's mercy,
the rainbow signs of the peace of Christ,
one in his love, we proclaim his love's promise:
fulfilled when creation is one.
So we glorify God,
known as crucified Lord;
in the Spirit of love,
endlessly adored.

© 1991 Stainer & Bell Limited

Written: 31 August 1990.

Suggested tune: LAKE ROAD.

LAKE ROAD   *Raymond Clarke (1925 -)*

Called to one faith and re – ceiv – ing one Spi – rit, we share one hope in the

peace of Christ; com–ing as sis–ters and broth–ers to–geth–er, we

pray that the church_____ may be one. We all serve the one God,

known as cru–ci–fied Lord; in the Spi – rit of

love, end – less–ly a – dored.

80

8.7.8.7.D.

Based on Luke 7, 36-50

Yes, the woman was a sinner;
such a scandalous affair!
first she wet his feet with weeping,
then she dried them with her hair;
Then she kissed them with such fervour,
in the most abandoned way;
then just drenched them with her perfume:
such a mannerless display!

Simon saw her sin so clearly,
from the pharisaic view;
thought, if he had been a prophet,
Jesus would have seen it too.
See her, coldly courteous Simon,
in your tight-reined purity:
she, abundantly forgiven,
shows her love abundantly.

Jesus, coldly we receive you,
in our self-esteem and pride:
judging you, by judging others,
sternly thrusting you aside.
Come, surprise us with forgiveness;
let our love for you increase;
teach us mercy, as you tell us:
'faith has saved you, go in peace'.

Written: 10 August 1990.

Suggested tunes: WÜRZBURG or NETTLETON or NORMANDY (Bost).

81

10.10.10.10.

For Albert Ernest Gaunt, born 7 September 1900, died 1968, in whom I discovered the 'fatherhood' of God.

Based on Ephesians 3, 14-21

Eternal God, from whose eternal love
is formed one family in heaven and earth,
make us your answer to our prayers for peace,
receiving every person at Christ's worth.

Out of the riches of your glory, give
your strengthening Spirit, gentle as a dove,
who comes with Christ, to fill our hearts with faith
and root and ground us firmly in your love.

Bring us, with all your saints, to comprehend
eternal breadth and length and depth and height,
to know the past-all-knowledge love of Christ
and share your fullness in eternal light.

To you, all-loving God, whose power in us
will far exceed our faith's expectancy,
to you be glory in the Church, in Christ,
from age to age and to eternity!

Written: 7 September 1990.

Suggested tunes: BOROUGH or HOLBORN.

104

82

11.11 and Chorus 5.5.6.5.

Based on John 11, 20-37

Martha, meeting Jesus, looked at him and said,
'had you come, my brother never would have died.'
Strange was the answer:
'die with me and live;
live with me, believing;
never ever die!'

Jesus, seeing Mary weeping, shared her grief;
felt, in his own spirit, death at war with life.
Strange was his answer:
'die with me and live;
live with me, believing;
never ever die!'

Jesus wept, and some said, 'how he loved his friend!'
'This man should have saved him,' others then complained.
Strange was his answer:
'die with me and live;
live with me, believing;
never ever die!'

Christ, our Resurrection, dying on the cross;
Christ, our Life: we welcome your life-giving voice.
Strange is your promise:
we shall never die,
we, who live believing,
die with you and live!

Written: 15 November 1990.

Suggested tune: NOEL NOUVELET.

83

8.6.8.6.D. and Chorus

The Jews, God's chosen people, sing
their song of faith and praise;
and no distress has silenced yet
the endless song they raise;
God's chosen people have endured
deep torment down the years;
and yet, through torture, pain and death,
joy springs from grief and tears.
We too are the people of God
whose song is never silenced;
we too are the people of God
whose joy can never be killed.

God's Word made flesh for us, in Christ,
who was himself a Jew,
despised, rejected, crucified,
makes us God's people too.
The sorrow of his human love,
brings grief to all our joy;
and yet the joy we have in him,
no sorrow can destroy.
We too are the people of God
whose song is never silenced;
we too are the people of God
whose joy can never be killed.

We look towards the time when we,
and all the human race,
will sing the song and share the joy
and celebrate God's grace;
when enemies are reconciled,
and nations live in peace;
as depths of joy and powers of song
eternally increase.
For we are the people of God
whose song is never silenced;
for we are the people of God
whose joy can never be killed.

106

Written: 11 January 1991.

Suggested tune: ZEMIR.

Author's note: Inspired by words of Elie Wiesel, from *Four Hasidic Masters and Their Struggle Against Melancholy*, quoted by Robert McAfee Brown in *Elie Wiesel Messenger to All Humanity* (both published by University of Notre Dame Press, 1978 and 1983):

> 'Who is a Jew? A Jew is he — or she —
> whose song cannot be muted, nor can his or
> her joy be killed by the enemy . . . ever.'

cho‐sen peo‐ple have en‐dured deep tor‐ment down the years; and

yet, through tor‐ture, pain and death, joy springs from grief and tears. We

too are the peo‐ple of God whose song is nev‐er si‐lenced; we

too are the peo‐ple of God whose joy____ can__ nev‐er be killed.

84   9.8.9.8.

For the women of the Lancaster District Council of the United Reformed Church

Based on Matthew 5, 3-9

Great God, our poverty of soul,
is blessed with boundless wealth from you;
and yet to make the gift complete,
we know we need our neighbours too.

You comfort us in grief and pain,
and in the comfort we receive,
we too must share our neighbours' hurt
and comfort others when they grieve.

Through Jesus, dying on the cross,
as helpless as he was at birth,
his meekness in his neighbours' hands,
becomes our power to gain the earth.

Great God, whose mercy never ends,
make us as merciful as you;
your mercy blesses us, when we
have mercy on our neighbours too.

Each neighbours' mind and body are
like living temples of your grace,
approached in pure and holy awe,
to seek your presence face to face.

Bless us and, through our faithfulness,
let justice, joy and hope increase;
bring us with neighbours, reconciled,
to be the children of your peace.

© 1991 Stainer & Bell Limited

Written: 19th January 1991.

Suggested tunes: ORREST HEAD or FOLKSONG.

ORREST HEAD

Raymond Clarke (1925 -)

Great God, our po – ver – ty of soul, is blessed with

bound – less __ wealth from you; and yet to

make the gift com – plete, we know we need our neigh – bours too.

85

Touch me, touch me, living Christ;
touch me, fill me with your grace;
touch me, bring me back to life;
touch me, heal me, give me peace.

Touch me, heal me, give me peace;
touch my heart, direct my ways;
touch me, let me clearly see
every person through your eyes.

Every person, through your eyes,
I will see as God's own child,
whose despair and hope you share,
till earth's enmity is healed.

Till earth's enmity is healed,
you are constantly betrayed;
touch us, teach us, risen Christ,
never more be crucified.

Never more be crucified:
touch us, fill us with your grace;
touch us, bring us back to life;
touch us, heal us, give us peace.

Written: 17 January 1991.

Suggested tune: EMMA.

Author's note: These words arose out of the cry of one of Samuel Taylor Coleridge's sons, one night: 'Touch me, only touch me with your finger ... I am not here, touch me, Mother, that I may be here'.

TRANSLATIONS

86

8.7.8.7.6 6.6 6.7.

For Joe Seremane

From the German of Martin Luther, 1483-1546

God is our refuge and defence,
whose shield and weapons round us,
ensure our safe deliverance
from evils that confound us.
The old foe still intends
to gain his ruthless ends,
determined on his course,
and armed with cunning force:
on earth he has no equal.

Though we may strive with all our might,
we face complete destruction;
the one true man takes up our fight,
whom God himself has chosen.
You ask us, 'Who is this?'
Why, Jesus Christ! He is
the Lord of Hosts' own Son,
Our God, the only one
who triumphs in the battle.

If devils lurked on every side,
all eager to devour us,
we still should not be terrified:
they cannot overpower us.
The peevish prince of lies,
however hard he tries,
is impotent to hurt
and has his just desert:
the slightest word can fell him.

They must allow God's Word to stand,
and fall inert before it.
We trust the issue to his hand,
who gives us his own Spirit.
And though they take away
all we hold dear today:
wealth, honour, life or kin;
we know they cannot win.
The Kingdom shall not fail us.

Written: Easter Day, 7 April 1985, finally revised 29 November 1988.

Suggested tune: EIN' FESTE BURG also known as A SAFE STRONGHOLD, A SURE STRONGHOLD and A STRONGHOLD SURE.

87 L.M.

From the Latin of Thomas Aquinas, c.1225-74 'Verbum supernum prodiens'

The Word came in to time and space,
yet never left his Father's side;
he came to do the work of grace
until, as night came down, he died.

His own disciple, faithless friend,
betrayed him, and the others fled;
but he had loved them to the end,
and feasted them on living bread.

And now, in these two outward signs
of bread and wine, these means of grace,
faith feeds on Christ himself and finds
enough for all the human race.

114

By being born, he shared our death,
to give us life that never dies;
reclaiming with his final breath
love's crowning glory as our prize.

Lord, through your sacrifice we thrive
as, flinging wide the gates of light,
you give us confidence to strive
against the warring hordes of night.

To you, with God in Trinity,
our everlasting praise is due;
so let us live eternally,
at home, triumphant Lord, with you.

Written: 1 July 1987.

Suggested tune: DEUS TUORUM MILITUM also known as GRENOBLE.

88
10 10.10 10.

From the Latin of Thomas Aquinas, c.1225-74 'Adoro te devote, latens Deitas'

Receive our love's devotion, hidden Lord;
though veiled by symbols here, yet be adored;
our hearts are yours completely, through and through;
expression fails us, contemplating you.

Sight, touch and taste would fail to bring you near,
but faith perceives you in the words we hear,
and we believe through what God's Son has said:
he who is truth, speaks truth and faith is fed.

The cross still hides your power, as God, from view;
here your humanity is hidden too.
We trust in both, in spite of unbelief,
and crave your presence, like the dying thief.

We cannot see the wounds that Thomas saw,
yet say, 'My Lord and God', and need no more:
except that you will make our faith secure,
increase our hope and make our love more sure.

We here remember you, Lord, crucified:
the Bread of Life for us, for whom you died;
we come to feast from Love's eternal store,
and savour your delight for evermore.

Jesus, who served the mother-love of God,
immerse us in the meaning of your blood:
the yearning love, of which a single trace
absorbs the guilt of all the human race.

Jesus, as yet, faith's vision must be flawed;
give us, at last, a keen perception, Lord:
to see, unveiled, the glory of your face
and live, unblemished, in eternal grace.

Written: 29 November 1986.

Suggested tunes: SHELDONIAN or ADORO TE DEVOTE.

89   L.M.

From the Latin 10th (?) century 'Jesu, Redemptor omnium'

Jesus, Redeemer of us all,
before the first light came to be,
you were the precious child of Love,
at one with God eternally.

Love's light and splendour, shining still,
to bring triumphant hope to birth,
receive your people's heartfelt prayers,
which rise to you from round the earth.

Remember how, Creation's Lord,
you came in history, to grace
a virgin womb, and there took shape,
as one among the human race.

The witness day comes round again,
the time of year when we recall
your coming, from the heart of God,
by which you liberate us all.

The day when earth and sky and sea,
and all created things, unite
to greet your new-born infancy
with carollings of new delight.

We, too, so blessed since your shed blood
released Love's healing stream, bring mirth
to swell the universal praise
and fête the day that marks your birth.

Written: 4 December 1986.

Suggested tunes: VOM HIMMEL HOCH also known as FROM HIGHEST HEAVEN, FROM HEAVEN ABOVE and ERFURT (Leipzig, ?Luther) or JESU REDEMPTOR OMNIUM or EISENACH also known as LEIPZIG (Schein) and MACH'S MIT MIR, GOTT and SCHEIN.

90   Epiphany

L.M.

From the Latin of Caelius Sedulius, c.450 'Hostis Herodes impie'
('Crudelis Herodes Deum')

Why, Herod, so unpitying,
so fearful of the new-born king?
He seeks no mortal sovereignty,
who reigns as God eternally.

The magi, travelling so far,
preceded by his natal star,
have sought, with gifts, the helpless mite,
and humbly greet the Light of Light.

Baptized for us, the Holy One:
the Lamb of God proclaimed by John,
still comes to cleanse our guilt today,
and take the whole world's sin away.

Faith springs to being at the sign
of water turning into wine;
and all our glory and our good
are in the shedding of his blood.

Now Christ, your glory is unfurled
across the nations of the world;
in humble love, revealed as Lord,
you reign, eternally adored.

Written: 15 January 1987.

Suggested tunes: Proper Mode ii Melody or ELY or SAINT
VENANTIUS.

91

From the Latin: 5th (?) century 'Aurora lucis rutilat'

The light of morning sheds its rays,
the sky reverberates with praise,
the earth responds with joyful cries,
with lamentations hell replies.

Because the undisputed king
has shattered death and, triumphing,
treads down the evil that remains,
to free the wretched from their chains.

He, though his tomb was sealed and barred
and soldiers kept a constant guard,
takes pride of place in majesty
and leaps from death to victory.

The groans of hell are set at rest
and all its agonies redressed,
because the Lord, though left for dead,
is risen, as the angel said.

Jesus, our triumph and delight,
your Easter ends the soul's dark night,
restores the heart's integrity
and keeps us to eternity.

Jesus, at one with us, you died:
at one with God, now glorified,
one with the Spirit evermore:
one Trinity whom we adore.

Written: 22 January 1987.

Suggested tunes: SOLEMNIS HAEC FESTIVITAS or AURORA LUCIS, or (adding Alleluias) to LASST UNS ERFREUEN also known as EASTER ALLELUIA and EASTER SONG and VIGILES ET SANCTI and SAINT FRANCIS.

92   L.M.

From the Latin of Venantius Fortunatus, c.530-609 'Vexilla regis prodeunt'

As royal banners are unfurled,
the cross displays its mystery:
the maker of our flesh, in flesh,
impaled and hanging helplessly.

Already deeply wounded: see
his side now riven by a spear,
and all our sins are swept away
by blood and water flowing here.

See everything the prophets wrote
fulfilled in its totality,
and tell the nations of the world
our God is reigning from the tree.

This tree, ablaze with royal light
and with the blood-red robe it wears,
is hallowed and embellished by
the weight of holiness it bears.

Stretched like a balance here, his arms
have gauged the price of wickedness;
but, hanging here, his love outweighs
hell's unforgiving bitterness.

The Saviour, victim, sacrifice
is, through his dying, glorified;
his life is overcome by death
and leaps up, sweeping death aside.

We hail the cross, faith's one true hope:
God's passion set in time and space,
by which our guilt is blotted out,
engulfed in such stupendous grace.

120

Written: 5 February 1987.

Suggested tunes: GONFALON ROYAL or SOLEMNIS HAEC FESTIVITAS or VEXILLA REGIS.

Author's note: line 1 of verse 3, in the original, actually refers incorrectly to one thing that 'David wrote': *Psalm* 96.10.

93   11.10.11.10.

For Jane Pembleton

From the German of Dietrich Bonhoeffer, 1906-45 'Von guten Mächten wunderbar geborgen'

> As powers of good so wonderfully hide us,
> we face the future boldly, come what may;
> at dawn or dusk our God is still beside us,
> to whom we trust, completely, each new day.
>
> Yet still old torments cause us consternation;
> through days of fear and grief we have despaired;
> Oh, give our tortured souls, Lord, your salvation:
> the healing you have promised and prepared.
>
> Then offer us the cup of desolation,
> brim-full of bitterness, and we will stand
> and drink with thanks, in spite of trepidation,
> from such a dearly loved and gracious hand.
>
> Yet should you bring us back to share the gladness
> of this bright world, your sunshine breaking through,
> we would remember times of pain and sadness
> and offer up the whole of life to you.
>
> [As evening falls, the candles we have lighted
> will point us through the darkness to your light;
> we long to be with loved ones, reunited;
> we know your love outshines the darkest night.]

As silence deepens, let us hear the chorus
that harmonizes earth's discordant days,
poured out from the unseen that lies before us:
your children's soaring song of endless praise.

[By powers of good so faithfully surrounded,
secure and comforted in spite of fear,
we live each day with you Lord, unconfounded,
and go with you to meet the coming year.]

Written: 6 April 1987.

Suggested tune: INTERCESSOR.

Author's note: To give these words more than a new year application, verses 1 and 7 have been transposed. The brackets suggest which verses might be normally excluded. Verse 7 might be sung at New Year.

94   10.10.10.10.

From the Latin of Peter Abelard, 1079-1142

You make your way alone: a victim, Lord,
whose sacrifice will see death overthrown.
What can we say, so wretched, overawed,
when all the pain you bear should be our own?

The sins are ours, and ours should be the blame;
why should you suffer in the sinner's place?
Lord, break our hearts, and make us feel your shame,
for only such compassion shares your grace.

We see the anguish of the grievous night:
the evening came with weeping, which will last
until the third day breaks, and new delight
comes surging with you, Lord, when grief has passed.

122

So fill us with compassion: those who share
your sorrow now, will share your glory too,
and end earth's days of darkness and despair
in easter laughter, wild with joy for you!

Written: 1 July 1987.

Suggested tunes: CHILSWELL or SURSUM CORDA (Smith).

95

From the Greek 'Phos hilaron', 3rd century

Holy, joyful, glorious light,
pouring from immortal God,
heaven-blest Lord Jesus Christ.
Now the sun is set and we
hail the evening light and greet
God in Holy Trinity.
You are worthy to be praised
in our purest harmony,
praised for ever, Son of God:
source of life, whose glory now
all the universe proclaims.

Author's note: This text, written on 24 July 1987, will fit four stanzas
in the metre 7.7.7. if *heaven-blest Lord Jesus Christ* is repeated before
line 10. ST PHILIP (Monk) is the suggested tune for this form.

96

L.M.

From Augustine of Hippo, 354-430.

How blessed are all the saints, our God,
who having crossed the troubled sea,
have gained the harbour of your peace
and rest in your tranquillity.

Watch over us who voyage still,
with risk and danger yet to face;
remember all beset by storms
and hold them in your steadfast grace.

Our vessel's frail, the ocean wide,
but your love steers, and we aspire
to gain the peaceful shore at last,
the haven of our heart's desire.

Then we shall praise you endlessly,
great God, to whom all praise is due;
as you have made us for yourself,
our hearts must find their rest in you.

Tunes: TALLIS' CANON and SONG 34 also known as ANGELS' SONG.

97

10 10.10 10.

From the Latin of Peter Abelard, 1079-1142 'O quanta qualia illa sabbata'

Grandeur and glory those sabbaths attend,
which all in heaven observe without end;
rest for the weary and goal of the strong,
all found in God to whom all things belong.

124

There stands Jerusalem, city of light;
peace is unending and joy at its height;
there where fulfilment precedes all desire,
far beyond all to which hearts can aspire.

What of the king and his sovereignty there?
What of the peace and the pleasure they share?
Let those who know it the glory unfold:
if such deep rapture can ever be told.

Meanwhile, we lift up our minds to the heights,
setting our hearts on the city's delights;
coming from Babylon, there we shall be:
home in Jerusalem, finally free!

There all distress will be brought to an end;
sheltered in Zion, our songs will ascend,
endlessly praising you, all-gracious Lord,
source of all blessedness, ever adored.

Sabbath on sabbath there, ever sustained,
sabbaths unending and joy unrestrained;
joy past expression, to which we give tongue:
by us, with angels, eternally sung.

Endless the glory our God will receive:
from whom and *through* whom and *in* whom all live.
From whom as Father, and *through* whom as Son,
in whom as Spirit: eternally One.

Written: 22 October 1987.

Suggested tune: QUEDLINBURG.

Author's note: For a translation to fit REGNATUR ORBIS, see *'What of those sabbaths . . .'* (**113**)

98   Christen Und Heiden

10.10 10 10.

From the German of Dietrich Bonhoeffer, 1906-45 'Menschen gehen zu Gott in ihrer Not'

People draw near to God in their distress,
pleading for help and begging peace and bread,
rescue from guilt and sickness, nearly dead.
Christian or not, all come in helplessness.

People draw near to God in his distress:
find him rejected, homeless, without bread,
burdened with sin and weakness, nearly dead.
Christians stand with God in his wretchedness.

And God draws near to people in distress,
feeding their souls and bodies with his bread;
Christian or not, for both he's hanging dead,
forgiving, from the cross, their wickedness.

Written: 31 January 1988.

Suggested tune: STONER HILL.

99

8.8.8.8.8.8.

Paraphrased from the last paragraph of The Quest of the 'Historical Jesus': Albert Schweitzer

He comes to us as one unknown
as, by the Galilean lake,
he came to those who knew him not:
and speaks the same words, 'Follow me'.
He comes to set us to the tasks
he will fulfil in our own time.

126

As he commands and we obey,
he will reveal himself to us
in conflicts, toils and sufferings
encountered in his fellowship.
In our experience we shall learn,
as deepest mystery, who he is.

Written: 9 April 1988.

Suggested tune: WYCH CROSS.

100

8.7.8.7.8.7.

From the Latin of Thomas Aquinas, 1225-74 'Pange lingua gloriosi'

Here proclaim the glorious mystery
of the body and the blood;
formed within the womb, made human,
he the earth's transcendent Lord;
offered for the world's redemption,
promise of eternal good.

Gift of God, the child of Mary,
mother pure in thought and deed;
he enriched earth's conversation,
scattering his word like seed;
then, his time fulfilled, he gave us
food and drink to meet our need.

On the night of that last supper,
there reclining with his friends,
met to celebrate Passover,
eating as the law demands:
he, as food for his disciples,
gives himself from his own hands.

Word made flesh, by word is making
simple bread his flesh, and we
here discern Christ's blood, though senses
nothing more than wine can see:
faith alone, true hearts sustaining,
can perceive the mystery.

Therefore we, with deepest reverence,
celebrate this sacrament;
finding all the ancient scriptures
sealed in his new covenant;
what the senses fail to fathom,
faith receives as nourishment.

Praise and worship to the Father,
power and blessing to the Son,
honour to the Holy Spirit,
glory to the Three in One;
let the Church proclaim for ever
what eternal Love has done.

Written: 15 April 1988.

Suggested tunes: PANGE LINGUA (Sarum/Mechlin) and PICARDY
also known as FRENCH CAROL.

101
8.7.8.7.8.7.

From the Latin of Venantius Fortunatus, c.530-609 'Pange lingua gloriosi'

Here proclaim the glorious battle
and the deadly conflict fought;
celebrate the cross, the glory,
and the noble triumph wrought,
as the world's Redeemer conquered
through the sacrifice he brought.

God, the great Creator, pitied
human nature's grievous fall,
as the fruit of guilty knowledge
caught and held the earth in thrall;
seeing that a tree brought ruin,
by a tree God saved us all.

Since the work of our salvation
made for this necessity:
that the manifold deceiver
be destroyed through Calvary;
so, from wounds that foe inflicted,
flows the certain remedy.

So, at last, there came the fullness
of the sacred time when he,
author of the whole creation,
came from God's eternity,
clothed in flesh, the child of Mary,
in divine humility.

Then, with thirty years completed,
willingly and open-eyed,
dedicated to his purpose,
nothing turning him aside:
born to be the Lamb for slaughter,
lifted on the cross he died.

Vinegar and gall, the spitting,
piercing nails, and then the spear
thrust into his gentle body;
earth and ocean, every sphere
will be cleansed by blood and water
from the river flowing here.

Tree of faith, among all others
none so noble, none so great;
not another in the forest
bears such leaves, such flowers or fruit;
wood and nails become so precious,
bearing such a precious weight.

Towering tree, now bend your branches,
let compassion, reaching wide;
soften all your normal hardness
as your nature is belied;
holding there the king of heaven,
gently tend him, crucified.

You alone, throughout the ages,
had the honour to prepare
sheltered harbour for earth's pilgrims*,
wrecked and sunk in our despair;
by the Lamb's shed blood anointed,
his the holiness you share.

Praise to the eternal Father,
praise to the eternal Son,
praise to the eternal Spirit,
honour to the Three in One;
praise the Love that has redeemed us;
publish all God's grace has done.

*literally: sailors

Written: 24 April 1988.

Suggested tune: PICARDY also known as FRENCH CAROL.

102

7.6.7.6.D.

From the German of Paul Gerhardt, 1607-76 'O Haupt voll Blut und Wunden'

O wounded head, enduring
such bitter grief and scorn,
so racked by pain and bleeding
with piercing crown of thorn;
once crowned with light and reigning
in noblest majesty,
though now condemned and dying,
still hailed as Lord by me.

My Lord, you condescended
to bear my weight of shame;
for sins I have committed
you shoulder all the blame.
See, here I stand, a sinner
who should hang in your place;
yet give me, my Redeemer,
the vision of your grace.

My heart is overflowing
with thanks, my dearest friend;
and, through your death, discerning
the good that you intend,
I dare to ask, Lord, make me
as true as you are true,
and when death overtakes me
my life will end with you.

Come, when my life is over,
my confidence and shield,
and by your cross, my Saviour,
my guilt will all be healed;
then I will gaze upon you
with trust no word can tell,
and know, as I embrace you,
who dies with you dies well.

Written: 31 January 1988.

Tune: PASSION CHORALE also known as O HAUPT VOLL BLUT UND WUNDEN or HERZLICH THUT MICH VERLANGEN.

103

L.M.

From the Latin of Aurelius Prudentius Clemens, 348-413

Go, night and darkness, sullen cloud,
all earthly turmoil and dismay;
see, where the distant sky shows white:
now Christ is come, so fly away!

The gloomy veil is torn aside,
and riven by the sun's bright sword,
and all earth's colour is revived,
lit by the glory of the Lord.

Our darkness, too, will be dispersed,
the guilty conscience pierced with light;
our secret thoughts will be revealed:
laid open to our sovereign's sight.

Great Lord, whose light has searched us out,
sustain and grant our heart's desire,
to see our sin and self-deceit
consumed in your refining fire.

Made one with us, so long ago,
in Jordan, where you were baptized;
you lift us now towards your light,
where all our hopes are realized.

Written: 23 November 1989.

Suggested tunes: SAMSON and DEVONSHIRE (Lampe) also known as INVITATION (Lampe) or KENT (Lampe).

104

8.7.8.7.4.7.

From the Welsh of William Williams and a literal translation by John Richards

Lead me, God, across the desert,
this poor pilgrim, still a slave;
having neither life nor vigour,
lost already in the grave.
Mighty Saviour,
you can raise me from the dead!

Let the fiery pillar lead me
on by night; the cloud by day.
Hold me in your hands securely,
as I travel life's rough way.
Send me manna,
so that I may not despair.

Open up sweet wells of water
from the rock's unyielding face;
through life's desert let me follow
your clear stream of saving grace.
Grant this favour,
till I share your full delight.

Though I cross the river Jordan,
by death's fearsome power dismayed;
you have come this way before me:
why, then, should I be afraid?
Through the torrent,
I will shout your victory!

I will trust your grace, my Saviour;
praise the conquest you have won:
you have trampled hell and Satan;
all death's powers have been undone!
Hill of Calvary:
may it never leave my mind.

Written: 3 October 1988.

Suggested tunes: CWM RHONDDA and CAPEL-Y-DDOL.

105

10 10.10 10.10 10. and chorus 10 10.

From the Welsh of W. Rhys Nicholas and a literal translation by John Richards

Great Son of God, your miracle in me,
has filled my life with joy and set me free;
you held me by your Spirit all along;
and while life lasts, I mean to sing my song:
for even now, I see your beauty shine
and thrill to feel its boundless glory mine.
The alleluia fills my being, Lord,
for you, my Jesus, endlessly adored!

You are my day's bright sun, Christ crucified,
whose beauty spreads its glory far and wide;
your dawning scatters night's uncertainty;
I once was blind, but you have made me see!
At one with you, my world is full of light;
in your communion, joy is at its height.
The alleluia fills my being, Lord,
for you, my Jesus, endlessly adored.

All praise is due to you, all holy Lord;
in you life's hope and purpose are restored;
your living Word has filled the empty void;
the great abyss between us is destroyed;
Creation's music, Mary's Son, now rings,
and for your beauty every mountain sings. *
The alleluia fills my being, Lord,
for you, my Jesus, endlessly adored.

Written: 2 December 1988.

Suggested tune: PANTYFEDWEN (M. Eddie Evans).

Author's note: * in my perception every mountain sings.

106

5.5.6.5.6.5.6.5. and chorus.

From the French of Edmond Louis Budry, 1854-1932 'A toi la gloire'

Yours is the glory,
Resurrected One;
yours the final victory,
God's eternal Son.
Now the angel greets you,
sweeping through death's night;
moves the stone that guards you,
floods the grave with light.
Yours is the glory,
Resurrected One;
yours the final victory,
God's eternal Son.

See his appearing,
with the wounds he bore;
see your Saviour, living:
see, and doubt no more!
Enter into gladness,
people of the king;
let delight be endless:
Christ is triumphing!
Chorus

Fear flies before him!
He whom we adore,
once death's helpless victim,
lives for evermore.
Prince of Peace: our victory,
life and strength are here,
flooding us with glory;
no, we shall not fear!
Chorus

Written: 1988.

Suggested tune: MACCABAEUS.

107

8.7.8.7.8.7.

Adapted from the liturgy of St James

Mortal flesh, in breathless wonder
and with trembling awe, come near;
by no earthly thought distracted,
contemplate the presence here
of the Living Bread from heaven:
Christ, the Lord, whom we revere.

Glorious king of endless ages,
dwelling in God's holiness;
loving human nature dearly,
grieving for our wickedness;
formed within the womb of Mary,
born to bear our wretchedness.

Praised by all the hosts of heaven;
praised by all created things;
every righteous soul, each prophet,
martyr and apostle sings,
'Praise and glory in the highest,
glory to the King of kings!'

Six-winged Seraphim extol him,
veil their faces over-awed;
cherubim, all-seeing, praise him:
'Holy, holy, holy, Lord!
Alleluia! Alleluia!
Christ, eternally adored!'

Another version of verse 1:

Let all mortal flesh keep silence
and with breathless awe come near;
contemplate the Lord of heaven,
present with his people here;
in the bread and wine receive him,
Christ, the Lord, whom we revere.

Written: 1988.

Suggested tune: PICARDY also known as FRENCH CAROL.

108   7 7.6.7 7.8.

From the German of Paul Gerhardt, 1606-76 'Nun ruhen alle Wälder'

The night is fast approaching,
its darkness is encroaching
on city, field and wood;
but I must be untiring,
through my dark night aspiring
to find in God my only good.

The sun has now retreated,
the day has been defeated
by daylight's foe, the night;
but in my heart is dawning
an ever brighter morning,
whose sun is Jesus, my delight.

My mind and body turning
from daily toil, are yearning
for rest and sleep's release,
and yet my heart is leaping
above earth's strain and weeping,
to find in Christ unbroken peace.

Spread your broad wings around me;
with your love, Lord, surround me,
protecting me from fear;
should evil overpower me,
or death itself devour me,
your child is safe, for you are here.

My dear ones too, though crying
in grief or pain, though dying,
or lost in boundless night,
shall sleep in your protection
and wake to resurrection,
rejoicing in eternal light.

Written: 19 May 1989.

Suggested tune: INNSBRUCK also known as O WELT ICH MUSS DICH LASSEN or ISAAK.

109 Easter Sequence

From the Latin ascribed to Wipo, chaplain to Emperors Conrad II and Henry III, d.1050

Praise the slaughtered victim,
Christians in your hearts adore him;
the Lamb has set the sheep free!
Christ, the guiltless one, now see
drawing sinners, reconciled, around him.

Death and life have fought it out;
their fierce conflict brought about
the end of death and strife,
the reign of life.

Speak and tell us Mary,
what you saw along the way.

138

'The tomb of Christ who lives again,
and the glory of his resurrection;
angels testifying;
the cloth and grave-clothes lying.
Christ my Hope has risen today,
and goes before you into Galilee.'

Come one and all and make your trust in Mary's word complete;
the truth she utters scatters all deceit.
Christ our Lord is risen now, indeed.
Greet his mercy, singing!
From your death, Lord, new life is springing.

Suggested tune: Proper plainsong melody.

110   11 11.11 11.

*Translated from the Latin of Peter Abelard, 1079-1142 'Advenit veritas,
umbra praeteriit'*

Truly, he comes to us: darkness is ended;
now night is over, his light is ascended:
ultimate sunrise, that floods all creation,
bringing his secret from death's desolation.

Night has made way for the great proclamation,
morning has broken, with songs of elation;
Christ comes in light from the depths of his prison,
Death is abandoned, and Jesus is risen.

Stripped of the grave-clothes, the body now glorious,
rises immortal, for ever victorious;
come to fulfil all the prophets have spoken;
promise of life that will never be broken.

Weeping is over, and death is defeated,
life is recovered and joy is completed;
guards, at the sepulchre, scatter before him.
Jesus is risen, and angels adore him.

Highest, Most Holy, once lost and forsaken:
now, from the sleep of the dead you awaken;
Angels appear at the tomb with the story:
'He is not here, but is risen in glory'.

Give God the glory and glad adoration,
from whom and *through* whom and *in* whom, creation
looks for the joy which, in Christ, we inherit:
praising the Father, the Son and the Spirit!

Written: 4 April 1990.

Suggested tune: REGNATOR ORBIS also known as O QUANTA QUALIA.

111   7.7.7.7.7 7.

From the Latin of Peter Abelard, 1079-1142 'Christiani, plaudite'

Christians, celebrate and praise;
greet the resurrected Lord,
who, as conqueror of death,
enters on his endless reign:
Christ, who wins the victory,
coming now, to set us free.

Reigning over all, supreme;
greet the resurrected Lord:
he has devastated hell
by his humble sacrifice;
all the angel hosts now raise
their exultant songs of praise!

Now deceit has been deceived;
greet the resurrected Lord:
though confined in mortal flesh,
scorned, condemned and crucified,
Christ transformed the human race
with his death-defying grace.

Once a captive here on earth:
greet the resurrected Lord;
now he rules the universe;
now all heaven sings for joy;
soon the earth and sky will ring,
with the joyful praise we bring.

God be praised, for our new birth
in the resurrected Lord;
Christ be praised: you set us free
in the Holy Spirit's power:
Mighty Spirit, fill our days
with undying joy and praise.

Written: 6 July 1990.

Suggested tunes: NORICUM or ENGLAND'S LANE.

112

8 8 6.D.

From the Welsh of William Williams and a literal translation by John Richards

Eden, I well remember you,
where blessings gathered like the dew;
and, though I fell from grace,
my crown was given back to me
by victory on Calvary:
I sing my endless praise.

Faith, see the place and see the cross:
the Prince of Heaven bore this loss
for me, in love unpriced;
The dragon fought the Holy One;
where two were wounded, one alone
has triumphed, he is Christ!

Written: 30 October 1990.

Suggested tune: ST. JOHN (Welsh).

113

10 11.10 11.

From the Latin of Peter Abelard, 1079-1142 'O quanta qualia illa sabbata'

What of those sabbaths? what glory! what grandeur!
kept by the saints in celestial splendour:
rest for the weary, reward of endurance;
God, all in all, as their joyful assurance!

There in Jerusalem, past comprehending,
peace is perfected and joy never ending;
there where fulfilment precedes aspiration,
always exceeding the heart's expectation.

What of the monarch there, what of the treasure,
what of the peace, of the rest and the pleasure?
How can they tell us the rapturous story:
those who encounter ineffable glory!

Meanwhile, we wait for the great celebration,
making our way to our true destination:
coming from Babylon, exile and sadness,
home to Jerusalem, city of gladness.

142

There all distress will be done with for ever;
there we will sing songs of Zion, and never
never cease praising; our songs ever soaring,
praising you, Lord, and for ever adoring.

Sabbath on sabbath, in endless succession;
sabbaths unending, delight past expression;
joy unrestrained, and eternity ringing:
we, with the angels, eternally singing!

Give God the glory and glad adoration,
from whom and *through* whom and *in* whom, creation
comes into being, with us to inherit
joy in the Father, the Son and the Spirit.

© 1991 Stainer & Bell Limited

Written: 14 July 1990.

Suggested tune: REGNATOR ORBIS also known as O QUANTA QUALIA.

114

8.7.8.7.7 7.

From the German of Johann Scheffler, 1624-77

Love, who made me in your likeness,
to your image forming me;
Love, who showed such gentle kindness
when I fell, restoring me:
Love, I give myself to be
one with you, eternally.

Love, to whom my life was precious,
long before I came to birth;
Love, for ever human with us,
born to share our life on earth:
Love, I give myself to be
one with you, eternally.

Love, for me, you came to suffer,
and, at last, were crucified;
Love, with you, I live for ever,
joy is endless at your side:
Love, I give myself to be
one with you eternally.

Love, my Life, my Truth, my Splendour,
Living Spirit, Mighty Word;
Love, by whose full self-surrender
my heart's wholeness is restored:
Love, I give myself to be
one with you eternally.

Love, whose yoke is laid upon me
liberating life and mind;
Love, whose grace has overcome me,
here is freedom, unconfined:
Love, I give myself to be
one with you eternally.

Love, your love's immense compassion,
pleads my cause at God's right hand;
Love, redeemed from condemnation,
in your strength, though weak, I stand:
Love, I give myself to be
one with you eternally.

Love, you are my Resurrection,
come to call me from the dead;
Love, I share, in your perfection,
glory that can never fade:
Love, I give myself to be
one with you eternally.

Written: 1 January 1991.

Suggested tune: GOTT DES HIMMELS.

144

Index of First Lines

Index of Tunes

*Where the tune is printed in this book, * follows the number.*

Index of Metres

Subject Index

GOD

JESUS CHRIST

THE HOLY SPIRIT

6, 16, 33, 75, 77, 78

THE CHURCH'S WORSHIP

Infant Baptism, Dedication or Blessing 12, 20
Believers' Baptism 1, 5, 7, 25, 27, 31, 38, 39, 52, 55, 56, 78, 85, 99, 103, 105, 114
Eucharist/Holy Communion 7, 46, 53, 61, 62, 77, 87, 88, 100, 107
Marriage 15, 52
Funeral 14, 96, 104, 108
Confession 8, 17, 33, 36, 40, 41, 47, 51, 66, 73, 75, 80
Prayers for Help 1, 3, 8, 22, 31, 42, 48, 78, 81, 84, 85, 93, 96, 104
Intercession 22, 24, 33, 40, 42, 47, 48, 69, 76, 96
Praise 5, 19, 27, 29, 32, 38, 45, 54, 58, 60, 61, 62, 63, 67, 68, 77, 95, 97, 105, 106, 107, 111, 113

CHRISTIAN LIFE AND WITNESS

Discipleship and Commitment 3, 4, 5, 6, 7, 8, 9, 11, 13, 16, 18, 22, 23, 26, 28, 30, 31, 37, 39, 41, 42, 43, 47, 49, 50, 51, 53, 55, 58, 59, 63, 65, 69, 72, 73, 76, 78, 79, 81, 83, 84, 85, 93, 94, 99, 114
Suffering 7, 26, 30, 35, 36, 48, 50, 54, 56, 60, 64, 70, 72, 73, 83, 86, 93, 96, 98, 104, 108
Reconciliation and Unity 2, 8, 22, 24, 52, 54, 59, 70, 73, 76, 79, 81, 83, 84, 85
Justice and Peace 2, 8, 22, 24, 31, 33, 36, 40, 41, 42, 43, 47, 51, 66, 69, 79, 80, 83, 84
Eternal Life 1, 6, 14, 25, 28, 29, 34, 35, 38, 39, 45, 49, 54, 55, 56, 58, 59, 60, 63, 69, 82, 91, 96, 97, 103, 106, 108, 109, 114
Healing and Wholeness 34, 35, 48, 49, 50, 56, 63, 71, 73, 81, 85, 91, 98, 103, 114
Confident Assurance 23, 25, 34, 35, 39, 49, 50, 54, 55, 56, 58, 59, 60, 63, 72, 83, 86, 106, 112